The New World

Also by Suzanne Gardinier

Usahn: Ten Poems & A Story, 1990

The New World

Suzanne Gardinier

University of Pittsburgh Press
Pittsburgh • London

The publication of this book is supported by a grant from the
Pennsylvania Council on the Arts.

Published by the University of Pittsburgh Press, Pittsburgh, Pa.
15260

This book is the winner of the 1992 Associated Writing Programs'
award series in poetry. Associated Writing Programs, a national
organization serving over 150 colleges and universities, has its
headquarters at Old Dominion University, Norfolk, Va. 23508.

Library of Congress Cataloging-in-Publication Data

Gardinier, Suzanne.
    The New World / Suzanne Gardinier
        p.   cm. —(Pitt Poetry Series)
        ISBN 0-8229-3771-9 (cl. : acid-free paper).—ISBN 0-8229-5516-4 (pbk.)
        I.   Title.   II. Series.
    PS3557.A7114N49   1993   93-37788
        811'.54—dc20   CIP

A CIP catalogue record for this book is available from the British Library.
Eurospan, London

A detailed list of acknowledgments begins on page 141.

Photo by Berenice Abbott/Commerce Graphics Ltd, Inc., "City
Arabesque: From Roof of 60 Wall Tower, Manhattan," June 9,
1938.

Book design by Frank Lehner.

I am huntin' for a city, to stay awhile,
I am huntin' for a city, to stay awhile,
I am huntin' for a city, to stay awhile.
O believer got a home at las'.

—*Slave Song*

Contents

Book One

Book Three

Book Four

Book Five

Notes

Book One

To The City of Fire

If I forget you let my sleep dwindle
and vanish in the dark early mornings
Let sleep forget me until I learn
to keep you near and not stray and not rest
in my wanderings over your rutted face
How can you think it can ever be finished
between us Do you understand
how the jostlings and marketplaces
of any other city how any
meadow or china cup will summon you
dying my provenance eyes closed trailing
blood from the severed leg left in the trap
you made Do you think you will dance that dance
forever Listen There will be a night
when the steel din of your heartbeat will fall
almost silent when I will ask your clamor
from you and it will be given I mean
to stay I mean to last your rebuffs
betrayals trials of stamina and trust
I mean to part your smoke to sleep
my mindful sleep and with that strength hold you
and say the parting words over you
and listen to the manifold voices
of those you crushed struggle into speech
to give myself to help make what will come

Admirals

He stares south on his column over anchors
over the tree of heaven at his feet
on an island where the avenues divide
his hand on his hip one foot forward
Below in the dirty circular pool
dead leaves float among the dumb fountain
    spigots
In a tableau a sailor hauls a wood boat
ashore In the center Columbus
sinks under a royal standard and a cross
To the right is a tumult of vines and trees
hiding shadows The corrosive rain
has touched the image and blurred it From
    his post
he assesses the neighboring smaller island
of moored motorcycles Pedestrians
Prohibited pushcarts gyros souvlaki
a blanket spread with used magazines
The cars simmer and hinder each other
around the Circle the drivers leaning
and cursing The engines gutter and steam
and with their soot firings erase
the statue's messages which include
these words *A Cristoforo Colombo*
Donava Un Mondo Al Mondo and
a winged angel crouched his nakedness hidden
his hand on a globe fingers digging in

The Ghost of Santo Domingo

What I remember I will tell
as clearly and directly as I can
At the end of this testimony I hope
at least to be understood At most
I hope that these sentences will lift
the weight silence has forced me to carry
and allow the bones of my ancestors
peace Let it be so Here are the dreams
In one I want again to open
my wrists and throat and at last be finished
In another I promise him he is old
and will die and that I will see to it
that his feast days fall into oblivion
while my life although broken celebrated
by no one will go on and on In another
the cookfires' ashes are flecked with bone
Do you understand Before his arrival
these things drew me closer into the Circle
solitude nakedness to wake to sleep
to plant to harvest to touch another
living body to sit beside the dying
and the dead to move across the sea Now
none of these sacraments is free
of his thunder and steel and pestilence his
enterprise Do you understand

To Peace

When will you come The days are long the nights
damp and quick but many I am leaving
the light for you my traveler Where
are you staying tonight What stranger's fork
and cup and sheets press against you The rumors
that you were seen in the east have come
to nothing Can you not send a letter
Without you the hours will not balance
The summer burns and the winter snows
course through the streets and flood the low houses
Our neighbors' faces are battlements
but perhaps for you we have lost this name
We hunt each other underground
hold celebrations in locked chambers
sleep uncovered in the rain The children
no longer know your name or your features
To the youngest you are as near as what hides
under grave markers They have not known
what it is to live with you my elusive
my empty-the-plazas my stay-away
How will I recognize your counterfeit
Does the place where your foot meets the earth still keep
the same imprint Has your blindness become
more burden than gift Will you remember
the way Will you feel the light's warmth and come in

Our American Way of Life

Smoking a cigarette in a classroom
a woman is copying sentences from
a book *Our American Way of Life*
the page marked Practice for Citizenship
The white lights flicker The others have gone
I want to be an American
citizen she writes and smiles *I have*
studied the American Constitution
I have a pen in my right hand
Today is a beautiful day I can
read write and speak simple English There are
many cars on the street I am working at
here is a blank to fill *Red Apple*
Supermarket It is raining now May
I write something else I will do my best
to be a worthy citizen I
enjoy my work She lays down the pen
rubs her eyes and turns to the section called
At Work and reads *This is a factory*
Many men work in this factory They
are factory workers This is an office
These women work in the office They are
office workers Everyone is smiling
She is left-handed and her back aches
from hours at the market stacking canned peaches

At Work

Day is gone light almost gone torch leaves
blackening Dusk gives back the citizens
blunted and hungry nine hours older
Sleep falls on them in the subway over
suppers alone or in company blots out
sealed cubicles sealed windows fenced highways
to be torn or painted or swept or cleared
tokens to be emptied into buckets
insurance and advertisements to be sold
rolls to be baked at four in the morning
fish to be dressed and shipped trucks to be loaded
and driven babies to be birthed and borne
dandled and fed teased and instructed
On the marble wall of the Greater New York
Savings Bank it says If God is not in you
where is He The corner smells of piss
and cologne and insect repellent this
October evening The sooty leaves
of the adamant Norway maples at the end
of the block run together and make a single
shadow Under lit rows of magazines
hung in arcs the citizens mill at the edge
of the kiosks' outspillings curious
about what has happened while they were trading
time for the coins they leave on the tray

At School

Two boys are hurried into the office
of a school A man flings them on a bench
and leaves them For an hour two women
shepherd guests to their destinations
No one pays the boys any attention
One still makes dangerous arcs in the air
with his fists The other looks away
and whispers *I keep after you until I see*
your blood coming from your eyes That night
by the river bar two with the boys' grace
trade fake punches whooping One swings his leg
through the darkness between them Do the boys
still sit together in the locked school
Who finally turned a face to them judged
their dispute wiped their cheeks sent them back
    to their lessons
One man holds the other's foot suspended
then drops it and drops himself to the sidewalk
and hangs on his hands long enough for his friend
to pretend to leave and laughing return
The watchers stir and take in one sharp breath
when he springs from the pavement and swivels
    down hard
into a full front-facing split
The men clap and whistle and lift their drinks
His friend bows from the waist and calls to him
Okay Okay man I give up You win

Refugees

Every night she dreams of departure
from successive islands of suffering
There is no mainland There is no knowing
The depth of any one island's pain
until after her feet have settled on
the new and she looks back over the water
but the glare blinds and her eyes are tired
and already she can't remember
On each new island are the orders
in the barked opaque new words A nod
means No A wave means Go away A pointed
finger means here is the dirty place
for you to wait to clean to sleep to live
Each island has its ordure to be removed
food to be cooked children to be tended
and saves these tasks for its most recent
strangers its little-loved On her knees
on the floor or over the steaming heap
of clothes that are not hers by the crib
of the baby who is not hers and who will
not stop crying a sudden sweep of her hand
reminds her of a gesture from the last
island but it is gone in a minute
The one she stands on she calls This new world
The one she has left forgotten she calls Home

Citizens

There is no need for concern the Usahn
Board of Directors informed the Chair
They are sleeping so deeply no boot toe
can rouse them The patterns of their ears
have molded themselves to the patterns of lies
They are watching the blue shadows dance
They are purchasing big ticket durables
They are warming cans of food on hot plates
listing their character defects Groping
for their own bootstraps they fall on their faces
They murder themselves and each other in
the rush to the trough of intoxicants
They snort swallow and shoot into their necks
freedom made of needles and powder
They subside in corners They can't say
what happened an hour ago They can't
find themselves on a map Each is
an isolated province easily
gulled and conquered They follow the feet
of the sleep-to-work-to-sleep shuffler
in front of them When you stand they bow
Hungry they suffer separately When
you curb their questions they quiet Brandish
the Flag and they weep or bristle as you
wish Sir Brandish the Law they obey

In That Time

In that time there existed Sovereign States
demarcated by invisible lines
called Borders protected by Bayonets
blades fixed to the barrels of Guns machines
designed to let death speed and multiply
In some States there was corn in some tungsten
    or teak
in some plums or salmon in some Dysentery
and Dying of Hunger two ancient diseases
One exchange between States was known as War
Across Borders with Guns wheat became
    hardscrabble
Wine became piss sleep a sudden hand
over the mouth a dooryard a ditch
granaries pine boxes arms and legs empty space
Within each State other Wars were conducted
These kept within Borders and were called Civil
Crescent beaches asked terrible questions
of mud alleys Barricaded Estates
kitchens enough for entire towns
touched the bodies of tin and paper rooms
leaving bad dreams and scars for them to carry
and pass among their children and friends
Each State held its own people dearer
than those over the lines It handed out
booklets with their portraits It held them close
with barbed bricks Civil referred to these ties

The Shattering

Laura Fermi

I was determined never to marry
I planned to draw my life's comfort and savor
from the laboratory from hikes in the hills
from anger at the boys in black shirts
with knives in the cuffs of their coats We were
at school together He was fond
of killing mosquitoes with elastic garters
and padlocking friends' suitcoats shut
His father worked for the railroad They lived
in a large cold building by the station
He told me of how he had walked alone
past the winter hospital where his brother
of some small thing by some accident had died
He was fourteen He wanted to prove
he could overcome what the hospital would
arouse in him There were no laces
or flounces or pickles with him In the days
of our wedding journey he sharpened pencils
and looked into the distance dictating
his *licei* text and at night taught me physics
We first visited here in 1930
I remember the city jagged and joyless
gray at the end of meandering streets
never a fountain or square the sudden
night in midafternoon thunderstorms

and wine secret in coffee cups When
we left Rome I hardly had time at the dock
to kiss my sister goodbye *And this*
is what I dislike he said *because*
in parting I feel that what I received
and gave is lost and only a sense
of futility remains In '31
when Nella was born he wouldn't touch her
He called her *bestiolina These little*
animals he said when she ran a fever
ought always to be well One cannot bear
to see them suffer On Sundays with friends
we walked in the country near Rome or by
the sea With a slide rule or with his thumb
at his eye's edge Enrico calculated
the relative brain power of humans and ants
per cubic centimeter of neurons
the speed at which the swallows flew
and joked and laughed with the other men
when a woman spoke One afternoon
on a steep summer climb my cousin asked him
Are you never out of breath Does your heart
never jump in your throat No he smiled *My heart*
must have been custommade It is so much more
resistant than anybody else's

Leviathan

Leviathan many tentacles
Leviathan cover choke with bluff
Leviathan talk out it mouthside
Leviathan make every trigger
Leviathan up to it in blood
Leviathan General Manynames
Leviathan President Hundredflags
Leviathan keep the meetplace empty
Leviathan got many lookout
Leviathan backstroke in swag
Leviathan swallow up what due you
Leviathan suck up it own
Leviathan a graveyard covert
Leviathan deep-six it friendlies
Leviathan leave hair and bone
Leviathan a scrannel papa
Leviathan buy you wholesale cheap
Leviathan paper and green numbers
Leviathan hundred million footed
Leviathan say what shit you eat
Leviathan give you it pink story
Leviathan hide it rack roadshow
Leviathan fill the Friday packets
Leviathan real-real clean-fingered
Leviathan deal out ears and toes

To The Tribunal

PANAMA

There was a machine that opened the earth
This was in April In December
as you know the Americans came
in helicopters to the neighborhoods
at night They had guns in the doors They walked
flamethrowers into the streets We were not
an army After with bulldozers
they pushed many bodies into the sea
In the Jardín de Paz in April
they opened one meter downstairs in the earth
People were waiting to find someone
They opened forty meters wide I want
to tell you the smell and the people who
could hardly They opened all day from seven-
thirty in the morning until after five
To tell they had to look They were missing
someone We found plastic bags with pieces
missing someone with the bones of the head
to pieces One body had its hands
tied behind its back They opened another
meter downstairs The people who had found
their families went away There was one
bag with three children People used sheets
to carry and went away The others
waited One woman waited all day

Blues

Come here baby wrap your arms around
Come here baby wrap your arms around
Want to hear you make them happy sounds

Tell me in my ear where you come from
Tell me in my ear where you come from
Tell me every sweet thing you ever done

Ain't nobody but us here tonight
Ain't nobody but us here tonight
Sing me all your old songs It's all right

Incidents in the Life of a Slave Girl

Although it stands between the kidnappers
and me There's the baby's cry again
the third time this long night Although it stands
before the kidnappers and testifies
There the lamps are out They're all finally
asleep And testifies to what
I suppose I must call my freedom I don't
like to look on it That ache in my teeth
comes the same as he used to bring
with his lash-threats and filthy compliments
From beyond the grave he has his triumph
I was sold like stock The paper says
Harriet Jacobs and below the name
of my Mistress Owner Friend I don't know what
to call her and the three hundred dollars
she paid for me when I had written her
no Tonight my legs remember
their long confinement This chair will offer
no comfort no matter which way I turn
My dress is stained with milk and her children's
handprints Before I can take up the pen
and continue to tell this life each night
empty-handed I sigh and force away
the cadences of their voices their praises
and questions their gentle needle demands

Even the babies' beautiful reaching
even what she would call her love for me
is dangerous to what I try each night
with what poor resources I have to build
The pen's nib splits On one side she
and her well-meaning sisters stand to admire
my weakness the very obstacle
that looms at me at this night desk
They draw me nearer But when our eyes meet
my own face becomes wordless and strange
On the other side my grandmother rolls up
her sleeves past her free elbows and fills
her free house with the smell of baking bread
She takes me in her arms and sings away
his barbed whisperings hooked in my skin
and I am protected but more Understood
But this too is a dream and a danger
I must stand at the pen's point where the ink
sputters to the page such a small sharp island
miles from Edenton North Carolina
both safety and desolation and forget
the pale sleeping bodies in this house
the milky obligations that bind us
and wrap the free darkness close and summon
my cell and will myself back there and write

Where Blind Sorrow Is Taught To See

Rain shines black where the red-and-white-light-laced
street divides and becomes two The walkers
hunch coats over their heads but no rain falls
here Through the wall between us comes your voice
you who give me shelter for the night
Foot to piston fire to axle to tire
to street with rain between makes music
surge and ebb with each change of light This
song finds your window across our bridge
you who give me shelter for the night
When does a bridge connect and when
divide When the wind pushes further in
to this room the sill glistens Chimes ring but
softly Your laugh rises and hushes them
you who give me shelter for the night
Sirens slur their frantic words but here
there is no danger The buttons down my shirt
have all day held in my loneliness
I unfasten them invisible
to you who give me shelter for the night
The light on the page fails just outside
the window The sheets are cool and dry
The street slicks and chills split in two Your warm
arpeggios sound through the lath and plaster
you who give me shelter for the night

Democracy

Nothing hurts but the foot is insistent
The foot seeps The foot has never healed
The foot pierced and swollen will not be hidden
The foot will at all costs be included
The foot will unburden The foot will rule
waking and sleep until it's attended
Attention The foot has something to say
but no way of speaking The foot is sealed
and drums the ground in coded unvocable
syllables The foot has a story
the foot can't tell The foot draws near
to weeping to the silver abundance
of stacked fish to fire to amputations
to the trading of copper cocoa and tin
to the spraying of passersby with rounds
of ammunition to the transfer of deeds
to the spewing of muttered words from the tried
and vanished to notices of eviction
to braids of rawhide with salt-stiff handles
to turkey and cranberry suppers to
the holds of ships to forcings on rooftops
and on pine needles to quahogs and muskets
to blocks of auction and execution
The foot pats the dirt garbled growing
tired but not resting The foot continues

Soldiers

Water they ask as she passes among them
every northern night in years of dreams
she who walks her own city beside this city
of the dying and dead She had come to know
the lane where they lie on top of each other
the swell of land that now holds an abandoned
caisson and the gunners' bodies around it
the cornfield now stripped where they lie in rows
but that was before this dawn this day spent
in the cellar with the horse with muffled hooves
This is a new smell this a new smoke
clinging to the hollows so she can't see them
until they are at her feet whispering
or staring from heaps of soaked cloth whose only
color is blood She does not know how
to stop walking She looks for the pastures
the stone walls the peach and apple orchards
the turnpike the white laundry on the line
but they intervene this new evidence
of human care and invention She has
no water She has only her eyes
and her feet until dusk and past dusk walking
searching for the lost village of Sharpsburg
searching among the littered bank's hickories
for yesterday's shallow Antietam Creek

Memorials

Walt Whitman I lay on the grass today
outside the house where you were born
past International House of Pancakes
Whitman Jewelry Whitman Fences traffic
Within your unlatched gate it was quiet
but the doors were locked You were not home
At the center a grove of sugar maples
held dry buckets hung at their sides
and dry tap spiles Plastic trash barrels
spilled hamburger boxes onto the grass
I stretched nearby and imagined you
sliding bloody and surprised into West Hills Long
    Island
learning to walk across the wood floors
Around where you began spread circles
of citizens bargaining bearing ourselves
from automobile to marketplace
to bed to work and back again
Under our feet spread the smothered earth
In your yard the land breathed without hindrance
I held a familiar stranger's hand
We stood and looked in your windows postponing
departure over the gashed blacktopped meadow
Inside were a spinning wheel a set table
a hearth but not you Walt Whitman We
searched the grass and later each other for you

Migrations

The long migration is over We are
here on the islands by the deep harbor
Now our wandering feet will be rooted
Now our songs will live in these waters
Here is our home Here is our way's end
The long migration is over We are
here at the knees of the rose ice mountains
Now the mammoth fat will drip in our fires
Now the hunters' luck will live in these waters
Here is our home Here is our way's end
The long migration is over We are
here gathered under the great spruce branches
Now the birds' return will find us here waiting
Now our ancestors' voices will live in these waters
Here is our home Here is our way's end
The long migration is over We are
here by the river thick with sturgeon
Now we will dance in the upland meadows
Now the women's decisions will live in these waters
Here is our home Here is our way's end
The long migration is over We are
here we few under this sky's protection
Now this land's salves will cool our fevers
Now the people's dreaming will live in these waters
Here is our home Here is our way's end

Book Two

To The City of Fire

All this time I have never told you
except here in this secrecy
never told you the winters I have watched you
draw your coat collar close to your neck
or sit on the public bench and unwind
and wind again the rags that bind your feet
I have seen you walk to the river ledge
the torn envelope crushed in one glove
holding the office letter asking you
not to return None of this
have I turned and held your hands and told you
I have seen you sailing three feet above
the riverbank with your mother's hands
spread over your ribs I have watched you stalk
from curb to curb the divided street
bent and belligerent glaring north
and south to keep the cars in their places
I have seen you lean against bricks discussing
solvents and adhesives I have seen you cross
the dirt lots sown with car parts and weeds
carrying diapers and cigarettes
the dark hairs crushed against your shirtfront
and I have said nothing I have seen you
cowered under a raised hand trembling
thinking no one saw averting your eyes

hoping with inattention to speed
the end of humiliation plotting
a future of bulk and luck and revenge
Cousin I have seen you blink and stretch
from the cooled movie theaters in summer
the film still in your eyes I have seen
the humid evening take you up
put its fingers to your temples and throat
lift you to the bus steps and away
I have looked after searching the standers
for your dreamy slouch and I have never
told you my comrade filling a high window
with your elbows and chin and vigilance
or leaning in the flowershop doorway
to breathe the street's day before it is gone
my partner of the nights and mornings
unspeaking in no particle mine
but still my companion celebrating
with the stripping off of costumes and fatigue
how distant early Monday is
how near the late Friday afternoon
I have seen you Forgive me Even now
this page tells and withholds puts its lips
with words unsaid behind them to your cheek
cannot touch you or meet your eyes cannot speak

Admirals

———————————— *Verrazano*

Your Majesty We found today
a very pleasant situation
among steep wooded hills a large river
forcing its way from the north to the sea
We took the boat and entered the passage
and found the country on the banks
ample and fragrant from a distance
the inhabitants from what we could see
dressed in what looked like the feathers of birds
They ran toward us with evident delight
raising loud shouts of admiration
or so we assumed as we did not know
their language nor the meaning of their gestures
Suddenly as is wont to happen
to navigators a violent wind
blew in from the sea We were forced to return
to the ship greatly regretting to leave
this region which seems so commodious
and fertile and which we suppose must contain
great riches As we did not disembark
we were unable to plant your banner
on any palisade Please accept
my regrets From our pitching anchorage
we claimed in Your name everything we had seen
and will bear Your standard here when we return

The Ghost of Santo Domingo

I've set six stones in a row near the eastern
shore above where the tide can touch them
to mark the time gone since they took her away
My feet trace the usual paths past cooksmoke
the place where she slept But inside something
has changed I dream the night of her first blood
celebrated in the circle of women
dancing singing silence Then there is
rope and her nails and screaming pushed into
sand her perfect integrity torn
to scraps scattered over the waves Her body
becomes the body of our village then
of the island then of all land and sea
and sky we know and the hunters of souls
shake the stains of the bloody division
from their beards and clothes They drive hands
    from wrists
They split tongues and bury them but still
they tell and tell I saw everything My daughter
is no longer what I was taught to call
alive Neither am I permitted
to lay her with her people join the broken
circle I have each morning's watching
over the water where she disappeared
and these six stones set in a line whose ends
run from each other and refuse to meet

To Peace

Peace I have feared you hated you scuffed dirt
on what little of you I could bear near me
scorned you called you vicious names Every time
you have settled over an afternoon
a friendship a night walk my brow my sleep
I have lashed free of your desolate island
back to the familiar continent
Coward I have watched you buckle under
nightsticks and fire hoses You have
disgusted me slipping flowers into guns
holding hands with yourself singing to bullets
and dogs Who can speak your language
but animals and saints What history records
your triumphs Over what centuries
have you reigned Miasma Where are the stone
lists of those who have died in your name
In the land where you are loved what becomes
of the veterans of all against all How
will I clothe myself How will I eat How
will I teach my children whom to respect
how to find themselves on a map of the world
when I have so seldom seen your face
Tell me Bloodless Outlaw Phantom what is
the work of the belligerent in
your anarchic kingdom Where is my place

Our American Way of Life

Chapter Eight Going Shopping What is this
This is a television Television
TV What is this This is a video-
cassette recorder Videocassette
recorder VCR What is this
This is a transparent telephone
with components encased in shatterproof plastic
and last number redial What is this
This is a remote controlled compact home
entertainment system with five-band graphic
equalizer five LED sound level
meter AM/FM stereo tuner
fourteen station presets cassette deck
high-speed dubbing semiautomatic
turntable full-range speaker system remote
volume up/down control What is this
This is a talking alarm clock What is this
This is a toaster Mrs Rosa
wanted a talking alarm clock The children
wanted a television Mister Rosa
went to the store Mister Manda went shopping
with Mister Rosa They bought a talking
alarm clock and a television
Mrs Rosa was happy with the clock
The children were happy with the television

At Work

As she nods down into and up from sleep
on a bus across the George Washington Bridge
the sun glints in her eyes from the girders
Her left thumb wrapped in a plastic bandage
flinches at the edge of a piece of paper
UNEMPLOYMENT *Discuss these questions*
in class Repeat each word after the tape
The light crosses her face The black knot of hair
at the back of her neck lifts and lowers
with the waves of her tiredness *Al lost his job*
He _____ for unemployment The _____
decided to move the plant from this country
to Singapore _____ is cheaper in many
other countries US workers don't _____
hard enough Unions often go on _____
Practice these phrases "as a matter of fact"
"interest rates" "closed down" "let go" Her lips move
under her cheekbones' sharp ridges past tollbooths
past white Greek letters on the blasted rock
flanking Route 4 past Applications
Now Being Accepted at gas stations *No*
he's glad to have the time off she reads *No*
he's not looking very hard One strand
of hair wisps loose and touches her cotton
coat's shoulder *The people are in a long line*

At School

It's the first hot afternoon upstairs
in the library at Grand Army Plaza
Cars lurch and careen around the triumphal
arch their rackets and rank smokes rising
over the park through the open windows
over the bent scholars and their assistants
shining with sweat At one slick table
two boys sit one thinner younger his face
upturned to search out and gather counsel
The elder props his cropped head with a fist
Between them is an open math book
and a sheet of yellow paper on which
they solve the numbers' riddles passing
a bitten pencil back and forth leaning
together arguing conferring
If you want it the elder says *you have to
keep up your grades My mother she doesn't
want me to go in but I'm not up on
commercial planes I like small sleek planes Yeah*
he looks away from the page and the table
and his friend *You can have fun in those babies
Fire a couple of missiles Destroy
a tiny country What a feeling No
I'm serious* he insists as his friend
fidgets and giggles and flicks the pencil

into a spinning circle and then
onto the floor The newspapers rustle
A young woman puts one finger to her lips
When you want to go the younger asks
his eyes on his friend's face dancing away
then returning the numbers nothing compared
with this With love's demanding attention
he notes each minute change of expression
for an instant in his own face keeps it
then lets it go *Look* says the elder
tearing a sheet from his notebook The side
of his hand leaves a faint imprint as he draws
an airplane his lips pinched cheeks drawn taut
with the work of his passionate precision
The other boy sighs The trees and the cars
breathe alternately across the room
Beside the scrubby equations appears
the smooth penciled body the pointed nose
in the blind tapering forehead small windows
but no one inside The younger boy watches
as it appears Its fins and flanks
are smudged and erased and redrawn dappled
with numbers and chevrons with the striped and
     starred
insignia of the young artist's nation
the marked missiles tucked under its wings

Refugees

By the time the stars prick their faint patterns
over the steel peaks her eyes are moving
under closed lids the blanket tucked tight
the day's last questions answered forehead kissed
Her father is on his knees again
at the center of the circle of boots
and jeering the left knee of his trousers torn
his left cheek a red blaze over his beard
Beside him are a brush and a bucket
of urine Already the street is wet
and stinking and the knees of his trousers
and they spit and kick him to take up the brush
and make the street clean The light that falls
on the floor and pillow and her braided hair
is not from the moon and does not go away
but her eyelids' seal is complete Under it
come the suitcases and whisperings
the hot food served cold the haste the knocking
on neighbors' doors with fists and her father's
pale hand not taking up the brush curling
against his chest on the reeking pavement
Then she stands with her back to their five rooms
a story above the wet street All she wants
is forward and he insists with his hands
Turn around You will never see it again

Citizens

The trees have no leaves A man on a stretcher
is wheeled across Broadway to the hospital
his heart harrowed with bullets from his brothers
There he is John Doe There he is dead
To the people waiting outside in the cold
to whom the city does not belong
he has other names Implacable
Brunt-bearer Sentinel He who carries
three continents' dirt in the soles of his shoes
He whom the night marauders called for
He who looked on our lips and hair and kissed them
Omewale the child who has come home
Malcolm who stood by the plywood rostrum
and fell over the wooden folding chairs
This afternoon his solitude
passes into many hands The people
who could not protect him draw him close
his stained white shirt open at the neck
In the evening three women clean the floor
of his blood The tipped chairs are cleared A band
    plays
and those who know none of his names laugh and
    drink
The others still see him getting to his feet
to speak to imprecate and bless
You've lost your balance Come to yourself he says
You play music You dance You can build

In That Time

In that time before the Abolition
insoluble problems of burial
plagued the commonwealths The wars produced
more dead than the Directors had dreamed
possible Bodies piled and stank
fouling water blocking the thoroughfares
slowing the flow of commerce forcing
the living to walk with noses and mouths
covered with handkerchiefs interrupting
the public sleep with incessant chatter
The children although small individually
needed acres of earth in which to hide
The war dead upset their memorial stones
Burned they walked begging tins of unguent
or whirled as ashes in cones of wind
Drowned they surfaced impeding the shipping
importuning sailors with swollen blue mouths
Shot they lay gaping among their comrades
repeating the same chants as the others
Locate and fire on the led horses
In the window hung three guitars
The fire trench is deep and narrow
The mending basket was left in the rain
What is our place Where may we rest they demanded
carrying their intestines in their arms

The Shattering

———————————— *Stanislaw Ulam*

Adam slept by the pasteboard wall
away from the window all sweat and breath
I couldn't with the heat and the traffic
around and around the Circle below
I played my old closed-eyes game the march
of the single digits Zero the first
start and finish the column with no beads
One the Great Onion with all the others
folded inside it The Progenitor
Two the first separation and boss
of the body's pairs hot ears hot balls hot feet
Three the prime unbuilt and building I spread
Eratosthenes' sieve over my eyelids
19 31 37
41 43 Four the perfect square
that once mirrored the earth now only the winds
It was useless I stood by the railing
legs apart arms held out so no flesh
could touch any other There was no air
The jolt past one when the telephone rang
brought a brief coolness Adam didn't stir
Hurewicz said Hitler was bombing Warsaw
the planes and Panzer divisions erasing
the soldiers and their plumed horses and swords
Adam and I had just come from there

Book Two ———————————————————— 39

from our sister wrapping bread for the journey
our father watching our backs down the street
For some reason I worried about a square
near the house where a boy once pushed me
and I pushed back and our friends circled us
and all my courage bled out through my feet
his taut lips flecked with white I hit him
first at the edge of his drawn mouth Blood
spattered my knuckles and the breast of his shirt
and grief and cold joy coursed up my legs
His fear was the larger I was saved
I took him in my arms and laid him down
on the cobbles under my knees That night
I was sure the cobbles were powder the boy
dead Some curtain fell inside me There has been
a different meaning to everything since
The radio sputtered Roosevelt
This ruthless bombing of civilians
has sickened the hearts of the civilized world
I am therefore addressing this appeal
to every Government to affirm
that Armed Forces shall in no event
undertake the bombardment from the air
of unfortified cities I request
an immediate reply Adam slept on

Leviathan

Leviathan know that cotton river
Leviathan fit the holds with chains
Leviathan keep the count-house ledgers
Leviathan trade in backs and pussy
Leviathan own the sugar train
Leviathan stroll around the auction
Leviathan check you mouth and feet
Leviathan stuff you with it language
Leviathan cuff and cut you heelstrings
Leviathan annointed thief
Leviathan you days you evenings
Leviathan you heft and sweat
Leviathan lash and goad you faster
Leviathan solder all the doors shut
Leviathan filch you dividend
Leviathan split the stand-together
Leviathan fix the rise-ups good
Leviathan disappear the pickets
Leviathan gibbet the union talkers
Leviathan tighten the limey hood
Leviathan sow hock and coppers
Leviathan slaughterhouse reap
Leviathan wrap in the country banner
Leviathan break all the mirrors
Leviathan a hole-cut sheet

To The Tribunal

For seven days we were not allowed
to sleep They stood us against the walls
For the first five days we were given no food
We had to urinate in our own clothes
I was breastfeeding They beat my breasts
and the electricity there We were nine
taken in the night from the village
This was the season of the great rains
in Quang Nam province They shot the pigs
and buffalo and took us away alive
They kept my cousin in a separate room
Her name means The Smallest They took turns
    with her
This was the sum of the interrogation
There were no questions They called it
the gathering of intelligence
Many of our village had already died
We were kept chained in an ordinary shackle
in the form of a number 8 Our legs
and arms passed through the two holes One day
the Phoenix men the Americans came
They gave orders and inspected the shackles
I can't remember if by then my cousin
was dead Two days later the shackles
changed The new ones when we tried to move
bit our skin locking tighter and tighter

Blues

Lived here all my life Seen what you can do
Lived here all my life Seen what you can do
Ain't nothin about that story new

Way down is where my babies been sent
Way down is where my babies been sent
For writin on walls or late payin the rent

Lived here all my life Was a child here
Lived here Raised and buried children here
Seen enough bluejacket bullets to last five
    hundred years

Incidents in the Life of a Slave Girl

Dear Amy At last a moment I miss
the Rochester sisterhood tonight
This page is no company If I were there
I would tell you what is difficult to tell
here alone Dear Amy if it was the life
of a heroine with no degradation
But I am learning That is not my work
What would you make of this I am
no longer interested in virtue
The prison cottage my master built
miles from town and the lawyer's bed
and the cell above my grandmother's storeroom
bite head to tail and circle around me
Which of these snakes is most virtuous
I was sewing in the shade of a tree
at my grandmother's door At last I told her
that in one war I had been the victor
in the other defeated My master's campaign
had failed had proved against all odds fruitless
but I carried Louisa the lawyer's child
I had rather see you dead she told me
Amy this minute she stands at my side
than to see you as you are now a disgrace
to your dead mother Have I told you
My mother was Delilah the free

tavernkeepers' daughter my father Daniel
the carpenter They are buried together
The lawyer was kind in his own fashion
He promised to buy me and the children
My grandmother took my mother's thimble
and wedding ring and said *Go away*
Never come to my house again I can see
the leaves on the dirt the latch of the gate
Martha Blount whose husband drove my uncle
Joseph hounded back from the North
drawn and chain-galled through the streets hid
    me when
I made my attempt Betty the cook
spoke to me through the floorboards charcoaled
my face and fit the sailor's clothes *Put your hands*
in your pockets she said *and walk rickety*
like de sailors but the North boat did not sail
On the way to my grandmother's garret
Amy your windowseat is not unlike it
in size the father of my children passed
so near I brushed against his arm but
he had no idea who it was Dear Amy
soon I will leave it to you to decide
whether I deserve your pity or contempt
But I have another object It is
to come to you just as I am Harriet

Where Blind Sorrow Is Taught To See

Lips against lips The window is open

Your mouth deep Rain darkens the rooftops

Open The ailanthus is wood and water

Softly sucking Birds pace the terrace slate

Your tongue there Heat Warm wind crossing the sill

I am afraid The drape sashes loosen

Who are you stranger who will not let me go

Democracy

Where there was furnishing and canopy
is now plainness General Washington's pew
at St. Paul's is paint and varnished wood
On a brass plaque is his prayer this soldier
surveyor whom the Senecas called
Destroyer of Towns ALMIGHTY GOD
WE MAKE OUR PRAYER THAT THOU WILT KEEP
THE UNITED STATES OF AMERICA IN
THY HOLY PROTECTION THAT THOU WILT
   INCLINE
THE HEARTS OF CITIZENS TO CULTIVATE
A SPIRIT OF SUBORDINATION
AND OBEDIENCE TO GOVERNMENT
TO ENTERTAIN A BROTHERLY AFFECTION
AND LOVE FOR ONE ANOTHER Beside
the padlocked almsboxes the unlit candles
and the velvet altar rope a man
with no elbows in his shirt wheels a bucket
across the floor He stoops over the mangle
then heaves and sweeps wet arcs over the tile
In every pew of the sanctuary
is a man each separate from the others
one with cuts on his neck one coughing one
   stretched
facedown asleep one awake with his head
on his fists At half past ten they rise
and join the line for the tickets for food

Soldiers

After the war I will go to the highlands
and walk on the dropped red maple catkins
then on leaves then on snow After the war
I will hide in the swamps and watch the beaver
build I will walk where no human walks
After the war I will stalk deer empty-
handed I will eat wild leek and perch
and char butternuts and bake my bread
in the ashes I will grow peas and oats
When the earth turns the side I know full
to the sun and when it turns away
I will lie down near blackberry thickets
Until the strings of frog eggs on the pond
become gills then lungs I will wait Until
the larvae hung in the hackleberry
become little wood satyrs' eyed wings
I will wait until the brants and herons
and gnats and mud minnows depart and return
After the war the salt cordgrass will flood
and not drown Turtles will swallow ducklings
and snakes mice Milkweed will split and scatter
its continuance over the sedges
and violets and schist After the war
I will climb up to the chattermarked ridge
and sit waist-deep in ice till facing east

Memorials

At the Mohegan Diner off Route Six
a woman in a black apron sits
in a booth alone the delicate flesh
under her eyes lightly shadowed She holds
a cigarette beside her temple
and stares at the street but not at what's there
Behind her a flashing machine with a voice
mimics the sounds of artillery
Her eyes wander newspaper photographs
of the Memorial Day parade
At the edge of the cliffs near Bear Mountain Bridge
trees part for the academy of war
Inside the visitors' center are children
bickering trading some taking notes
to find Ten Qualities of a Cadet
Like fairness the teacher says *but don't
use that one Think of one of your own*
For the film we file into darkness
A smiling boy paints A girl in a lab coat
works by a flame In time the talk shifts
to the choice of the Profession of Arms
*A cadet must be prepared to defend
democracy in an uncertain world*
The children hush for the calm film voices
faces upturned to the flickering screen

The actor soldiers multiracial and cheerful
endure Basic Training as if it were camp
No one shrinks before screaming No one lies down
and does not get up Learning to kill
makes no change in the fledgling soldiers' faces
From there we move to the domain of machines
Cadets leap from airplanes cradling
stockless rifles They lay mines in the dirt
Through deserts they propel long olive trails
of ordnance Even the glaciers are marked
by the cleats of their boots At the end
there is music and the children applaud
Up the hill past brick houses and hammocks
still behind screens is the heaped museum
The children charge past the layers of banners
drums cornets the eagle standards of Rome
to the case marked Discipline and Punishment
where two reed whips hang together
one for faces used by Nazi guards
one from the American Civil War
In a sketch the Army of the Potomac
drums a coward out of the ranks
a sign bearing that word across his shoulders
Göring's dagger and baton hang beside
Hitler's pistol and Mussolini's hat

all labeled *Sic Transit Gloria Mundi*
Downstairs a mannequin stands by a mural
showing the invasion of Normandy
He is dusty His legs stop before they reach
his knees The card says he is wearing
black pajamas and sandals made from tires
Viet Cong Guerilla Circa 1967
He holds a rifle His eyes are closed
The children touch him and run away
to test the grips of mounted machine guns
and thrust their heads into cannon mouths
Around the corner from The Poles The Sword
and Protective Headgear suddenly is
a model of the Fat Man atomic bomb
Below is a letter to Roosevelt
from Einstein *This new phenomenon*
would also lead to the construction of bombs
as dawn leads to noon and noon to evening
and discovery to annihilation
Outside rock walls tremble with early roses
Three carpenters stretch and get to their feet
At the compound exit a gloved soldier
salutes every passing car On a bench
in the town an old woman hands on her knees
watches the fountain spurts rise and fall

Migrations

Far inland the earth under our feet
will welcome us without fenced farms or towns
To the west there is an end to our sorrow
To the west the deer are thick in the forests
The grandparents will protect us far inland
Far inland we will need no canoes
no weighted nets We leave them behind us
To the west the people of salt disappear
To the west the beaver are thick in the forests
We will be far from the forts far inland
Far inland we riding the turtle's back
will keep sickness away with our spring feasting
To the west we will die in our old age again
To the west the turkey will keep us through winter
Our young ones will not be taken far inland
Far inland all our divided bodies
will be gathered and danced for and buried whole
To the west our steel will make food and shelter
To the west the beans come too many to count
Our nights will be unbroken far inland
Far inland the bitter ones cannot hide
these stars from us these travelers' footprints
To the west we will tell the sky our visions
To the west the corn grows to the sun's cheek
We will carry our spearpoints and drums far inland

Book Three

To The City of Fire

Here is soot Today it is all I have
to give you My stores of honey and corn
and fresh water and even sand are empty
Here With this you can hold the city's
every corner under your fingernails
ground into the soles of your shoes riding
the pulses of your lungs' fragile chambers
traveling from your eye's edge to the back
of your hand Here is soot signature
of the city of fire and its web
of consequences It has spread its burned
body over the river filmed the slick
dark heads of the cormorants as they plunge
to eat It has settled between pavements
and the clothes of those who sleep on them
It testifies to the lost integrity
of forests of the earth's buried black veins
of tenements of poison sealed in drums
against flesh of circles of pointed tents
of the bodies of those who would not obey
or who slept on park benches unheeding
It is memory smearing the sunsets
to attract our shattered attention each mote
a crippled survivor voiceless haunting
our eyes and throats trying to find a way in

Admirals

October 1609 This land is
the finest for cultivation that I
have ever in my life set foot upon Miles
out we could smell it The people are
many and handsome after their fashion
not to be trusted but not to be feared
When they crept aboard to steal pillow slips
and shirts we dispatched several with only
their arrows' paltry resistance When we sat
to eat with them on the shore they insisted
we stay the night When we stood to depart
they thought we were afraid Each gathered
his arrows and in a great circle
they broke them and threw them into the fire
We are two days up the mighty passage
Three dreams will not leave me The first
is of one of their men toppling musket-shot
from a boat his chest opening then only
the river The second is of acres
of emptied land cleared for plowing every
rough place plain still that strong deep scent
The third is of a winter more severe
than any I have known The sun has gone
For some crime I have committed
I am cast from my people and left to die

The Ghost of Santo Domingo

All day she rocks forward and back whispering
the names of those who have disappeared
The ceremonies are now forbidden
She alone keeps the ancient compact
eyes closed one cheek covered with one hand
There were those staring outside the fortress
who could not fill a Flanders hawk's bell with gold
Their hands and their blood lay close beside them
It is her work to join them together
Her rasping grows faint but does not pause
There were those who fell before smoking muskets
There were those who shivered in fever blankets
and then were still There were those who were hung
over fires while they still moved and breathed
Her hands flutter She covers the burns with her palms
There were those who worked in the mines spitting
    blood
who curled into themselves and rushed under the
    ground
There were those who smothered their children
    and cut
the poison root and swallowed it
She calls them near and draws up the canoes
There were those the ships took chained and crowded
She scans the waters to see where they are
Back and forth she beats out the question
She whispers their names and makes offerings
for their safe passage from the bottom of the sea

To Peace

All day I search for you without success
None of the benches dividing the north
and southbound sides of Broadway holds you
and none of the fouled snow surging in torrents
into the sewers will tell where you are
My soles are tired and the sun is setting
over New Jersey streaming along streets
empty of the ring of change in your pockets
you who walk before the light gives its direction
facing the trash-blowing river wind
At intersections the fractious traffic
pitches and steams In the markets oranges
lie under their winter blankets still
Below the wood water towers and bare
unsettled rooftops the shadows of rising
smoke against brick walls tiers of windows each
framing a woman alone who stares out
below the ladders for escape from fire
the light stays longer and I say your name Here
beside steel-rimmed curbs and the rush of pennies
shaken in cardboard cups here below
unblinking streetlights and the later dark
I fasten my coat and walk looking for you
Here between the cobbled seasons I wait
Here above the subway trembling I say your name

Our American Way of Life

Chapter Twelve In School What is this This
is a school Who goes to school Everyone
Why do people go to school To learn
These are boys and girls They go to school
in the day These are men and women They
go to school after work at night They come
from many countries They want to become
citizens They want to learn about
the United States The teacher begins
She tells the class about Christopher
Columbus The teacher discusses what
he brought to America She lists
the others who crossed his ocean sea
The people leaning elbows on the desks
come from Senegal Liberia
the Dominican Republic Haiti
Lebanon Laos Vietnam
The teacher reads and describes how the Pilgrims
and Indians celebrated the first
Thanksgiving She tells about the tea
dumped in Boston Harbor against the taxes
It is nine o'clock They are out of time
I'm sorry she says *We'll have to wait*
until next time for the Declaration
of Independence and the Revolution

At Work

She ladles the grounds with a plastic measure
into the filter and snaps the lid down
pours the water sets the pot underneath
to catch the coffee stream The yellow-
and-brown uniform pulls across her shoulders
and over her breasts the yellow-and-brown
paper hat fastened to her hair He takes
the steaming plastic cup from her slowly
keeping his fingers there a minute
then leans on the counter With a damp towel
she sweeps the stray grounds into her hand
Donde vives baby he asks *De donde*
vienes smiling through a night's beard
No entiendo she answers her upper
teeth braced in plastic to teach them a new way
Where do you come from he says again *You*
want to know she asks *You never heard of it*
Tell me Cambodia she says *Y donde*
vives No entiendo Mister
she says hanging the rag on a hook
I'll teach you he says *Donde Where* She laughs
but *Donde Yes* he says *Vives Do you*
live Vives she repeats *Donde vives*
he says and she asks him back *Donde*
vives Yes he says *Where do you live*

At School

Excuse me the teacher says *Where are you going*
Mister Do you have a pass He nods
May I see it He sighs offers the paper
and stares out the doorglass laced with diamonds
of wire On his chest are a skull
and the words Harvester of Sorrow
The interrogation complete he continues
his journey She resumes her watch *Something's*
burning Charlie a colleague tells her
Can you smell it They don't know what it is
Probably toxic fumes she says *and we're all*
gonna die Nah Charlie says hooking
a thumb under his belt The buckle
says USMC *We're safe This is peace*
I did what I had to do over there
he says *I went and when I came home*
I lay in the streets to stop it I thought
I would change the world   I used to be
an idealist she says *It's still in you*
somewhere he tells her *No I don't think so*
Her gaze splits as another adolescent
approaches *When the revolution comes*
Charlie laughs *you and me Chickie we'll lie*
in the streets Don't hold your breath Charlie Yes
I'm telling you Chickie we'll lie in the streets

Refugees

Before the dawn before the rain started
before the men wearing helmets came
the people had made a place for themselves
across from the park at the edge of the Circle
Those who slept at night breathed under blankets
on cardboard boxes and carpet remnants
Those who couldn't sleep swept the sifted ashes
from the sidewalk around the barrel fire
and leaned back in split chairs the way they did
to gather the sun Before the bulldozers
there were bins of records and books spread to sell
and socks and plastic bottles of water
Some days there were gifts wedges of melon
birds of paradise with orange tongues
wrapped sandwiches a broom a red quilt
Before the police barricades to protect
those who sit to eat on the mild evenings
outside the food trucks there were other jokes
and other blessings There were bucket toilets
and dishes washed in the hydrant spray
There were towels and soup pots and cooking grates
Before the razing before the unmaking
before the quiet ragged retreat
a settlement lay at the end of the crosswalk
of cardboard of citizens of refugees

Citizens

There is chilly dancing in Harlem tonight
The babies kept up past bedtime are whirled
through the cold sidewalk darkness and taught a
    new word
Mandela who has walked from the prison free
Those who have told his story among them
whose persistent petitions have helped bring this day
pour news and music from uptown windows
and praise the dust road half a world away
that leads him from his cell to his people
who have waited for him since he was young
A mountain sways in the heat behind him
He walks gray and carefully his legs thin
In his hands one touching the woman beside him
one clenched and raised overhead in a fist
are all the defeats that have led to this moment
the bitter silent curling against blows
the ruined plans broken rocks in the quarry
his losses and what he refused to lose
the empty evenings when a message would come
and those that would not end and brought nothing
the secret betrayals from the distant kings
of the land where the poor streets tonight are alive
with the dancing of exiles singing his name
Now the argument is resumed with a bridge
between the dust road and the winter streets

In That Time

In that time after the Great Silencing
came the Age of the Empty Pedestals
Rope-girdled statues fell to the streets
or descended hooked from the jibs of cranes
Other objects of devotion appeared
in their places wet petals hills of clay
trowels paper parcels tied with striped string
ripped tickets spent bullet casings a list
of names each with a city beside it
an infant's spoon a cup of black milk
a metal cuff one violet slipper
a tooth a stethoscope a flute a flail
knurs of ginger an atlas of aquifers
a camisole a lintel beam epaulets
talcum nettles zippers fleece
a reed an abacus a photograph
of an old woman with one hand hidden
a girl with tortoise combs in her hair
the village committee those in front kneeling
a boy with torn clothes and an open chest
Notes were tucked into the stone crevices
Goodbye to you and your ancestors
I have a tongue I have a face
You are banished but remembered Do not
return Goodbye to the age of kings

The Shattering

──────────────── *HERBERT ANDERSON*

Wednesday January 25
1939 Dear Mr Strauss
I feel I ought to let you know
of a sensational new development
In a paper Hahn you may remember him
he helped open the chlorine valves at Ypres
reports that he notices when bombarding
uranium with neutrons a breaking up
This is entirely unexpected
The Department of Physics at Princeton where
I spent the last few days was a stirred
ant-heap Apart from the scientific
interest there may be another aspect
which does not seem to have caught attention
The energy released in this new
reaction must be very much higher
than all previously known cases
This might make it possible to produce
power But I do not think that this
is very exciting There is something more
I see in another direction
I still have this terrible fever More soon
Yours Leo Szilard In the evening
a young man finishes his supper
of boiled potatoes and lamb Blocks away

his elder seals the envelope
and wipes his cheeks with a cloth by the bed
Anderson stacks dishes and wraps himself
against the walk back to the lab
The vendors blow on their hands He remembers
from the afternoon the older men's voices
murmuring in the basement the restrained delight
in the hands that rested on his shoulders
Young man each in its own accent's music
Let me tell you about something new
Something in their faces haunts him
their kindness their most casual glances
etched with broken glass and trenches and kings
At the crest of the hill he turns and looks down
into the wind at the sooty lattice
of the dark island on which he was born
They have left the city He is alone
He knows that if he asks and listens
carefully enough tonight he will open
the secrets of every drop of his blood
every face every brick every streetlight-dimmed star
The room is empty He lights it and strips off
his coat to begin the interrogation
How can I listen so you will tell me
The cyclotron has been balking From

another experiment he retrieves
the radon and beryllium *What are you*
What do you keep from me He sits
by the ionization chamber he built
the uranium-coated plate inside
and opens his notebook At just past nine
he sets the source by the chamber and watches
the oscilloscope screen *Let me in*
Again and again there is a fracture
no one in his land has ever seen
The pulses of the new live thing surge
*Now large kick*s he writes *which occur one*
every two minutes For an hour he watches
and counts thirty-three risings without knowing
the name or the nature of what he is making
What are you He takes the source away
and waits twenty minutes in the absence
Zero counts He has entered the body
he cannot see and made fragments and fire
As he walks home he sees the fire locked
in the bookshops and diners and tailors' storefronts
the windows of oranges bandages salves
the gloved woman playing a clarinet
and still hears his questions *How can I know you*
and sees the jagged answering peaks

Leviathan

Leviathan ubiquitous
Leviathan touch every place
Leviathan hand on the channel panel
Leviathan 24–7
Leviathan hide it barrel face
Leviathan scepter make you jabber
Leviathan ducats make you sing
Leviathan hiss pretty fiction
Leviathan bribe you with cadavers
Leviathan jerk the puppet string
Leviathan Captain of Contusion
Leviathan Electrode Chief
Leviathan kick and leave no footprints
Leviathan debride it loyals
Leviathan break legs and teeth
Leviathan push and say you jump
Leviathan hang and leave you note
Leviathan skiver storytellers
Leviathan stitch the asker mouth up
Leviathan make you dig you hole
Leviathan scatter what you gather
Leviathan burn what you make grow
Leviathan the rabble smelter
Leviathan the marrow foundry
Leviathan Suzerain of Smoke

To The Tribunal

——————————————— NICARAGUA

I come from a village by the north border
The nearest city was Estelí
Now it is nothing One afternoon
after the ground had been plowed and corn planted
after the leaves reached almost to my waist
the soldiers came the Americans' men
with new rifles and new boots and new shirts
The ground was still wet but the sun had started
They stayed a long time We held our children
with one hand over each mouth so they wouldn't
After they burned the houses and the fields
After they stayed a long time One woman
There were black sacks of food after the burning
One woman Her father was a carpenter
missing one leg after mines in a road
She bent and picked over the sacking to save
the whole parts for clothes and they killed her there
shooting from the other side of the village
She made the children wood toys Cedar
grew there I learned cedar later I worked
in the hospital woodshop in the city
The air was cedar I am still coughing
I knew nothing I studied diagrams
to make knees and legs Then the people would walk
Cedar is light and lasts a long time

Blues

Leaves fallin down Here come the cold
Leaves fallin down Here come the cold
No face against my face no place to go

Where I used to live ain't nothin now
Where I used to live ain't nothin now
Burned sticks and broken bottles on the ground

Sundays we'd stay in bed and lock the door
Sundays we'd stay in bed and lock the door
Our clothes heaped up together on the floor

Incidents in the Life of a Slave Girl

Tonight I woke again afraid
from the dream of James in the cotton gin
He was here beside me He is here still
Charity's James by this quilted bed
It is the late hurried writing that brings him
his body lying in the machine meshes
four days five nights My hands ache They are not
strong enough to unscrew the press
and lift him out to wash the brine
from the cuts of the whip Shall I write instead
another life another story
where Charity's son James stood on the wharf
before he set off on his north journey
and after his travels returned there and I
on a morning walk heard a neighbor call
Have you seen Charity James is home
But he and his comrades who crowd my room
when I wake at night have no use for this
They want the truth as much as I fear
I have none of the strength needed to tell it
Is there a way this silence can express
what my poor pen is not capable of
I have had no sleep There are the first finches
There is the light on the windowsill
They are stirring They are waiting for me

Where Blind Sorrow Is Taught To See

It's Independence Day or by now
Independence Night I have waited for you
so long The day's heat rises from the streets
but the breeze will come if we pull the curtains
aside Show me everything We will have
our own speeches and our own processions
our own declarations our own pageants
of union But there will be no banners
and no militia Heard around the world
will be only this Each part of your body
is speaking a different language scapula
clavicle rib nipples soft then hard
against my lips In each language are hundreds
of dialects slangs speech rhythms and
impediments within each of these millions
of tones of human voice and inflection
My only hope of being able
to understand even the smallest part
of the conversation is to draw as close
as I can I turn you on your side
and run my tongue from the small of your back
down slowly over every province
between there and your navel on the other side
and back again and again and again
I listen I circumnavigate the world

Democracy

They took the beggar by the elbows
The cutlery shone under candles and lamps
The child's feet were wrapped and swollen
The greens arrived first pleasantly bitter
Her arms were tracked with scabbing and dirt
The wine swept against the sides of the glasses
She carried a bag full of empty cans
When the cloth lifted from the bread steam rose
Where she lived were planks and torn cardboard
There was roast duckling and tiny potatoes
There was part of a coat where the child lay
The city lights made patterns in the windows
They carried her She would not stop coughing
Over the hearth was a painted landscape
At the hospital they left her on a chair
The cart brought fruit and tarts and puddings
The child ate crackers from a plastic packet
The room smelled of meat and woodsmoke and
    perfume
She waited and dozed then took up the child
There was coffee and brandy and a violin
They crossed the city It took a long time
The elevator man nodded and smiled
Where their place had been was a wood barricade
Light snow fell It was a cold night
Light snow fell It was a cold night

Soldiers

———————————— *1967*

These five days and five nights there are no
lines at the offices of unemployment
no thin women stumbling across vacant lots
From the rooftops in the heart of the city
the curfew is broken by single shots
answered by blurts of machine-gun fire
in the dialogue of the insurrection
From the pawnshops they do not own the people
take televisions and jewelry and clothes
These five days they will not be beaten
or rat-bitten or cheated or sickened or starved
in silence These five days the world will know
At the corner of Avon and Livingston
on the sidewalk is a twelve-year-old boy
in tarred blue jeans and blurred sneakers
bleeding into his hands from his neck
Over him a Newark policeman props
the stock of his shotgun against his thigh
When the people rush from the tenements
he and his comrades club them away
A man who stole beer from a liquor store
lies dead The boy is alive From the ground
he stares and studies his city's foundations
a man open-eyed in a litter of cans
the policemen's gun butts and the blood on their
    shoes

Memorials

The tarnished band of old men slouches
sweating in the sun on rusty seats
on the steps of the soldiers' monument
The city has chosen this day to remember
those who have died for our freedom those
who fell on the field of battle to remember
Kevin J Dugan dead at twenty-one
a Green Beret airman in Vietnam
The hats and flagstaffs bob as the bearers
shift to find comfort to hear the parade
of speakers *A nation which forgets*
its heroic dead one soldier says
soon forgets itself Common good Brotherhood
The Monument stone's blurts of anarchic
curses and linked initials are silent
sandblasted to scars for the Occasion
Navy Commander Claudia Bates
says *There can be no liberty without union*
shifting the braid that shackles her shoulder
scanning the front ranks the fidgeting children
in uniforms eating potato chips *those*
who may have to sacrifice once more
One soldier talks about hospitals
given no money about soldiers who die
from drugs and alcohol and bad dreams

The marches sweep him back to his seat
Applause rattles up for the next in line
with medals and sweat stains on his stiff shirt
Legionnaire Richard Dugan the dead soldier's father
His son would be forty-two today
When he stands to read his speech there is nothing
He wipes his neck stares into the trees
and bows his head The microphone whistles
and a soldier strides on to read for him
When his wife appears weeping they hand her roses
A Gold Star You gave us Kevin Thank you
The bearers break the flags into pieces
In a corner a man dressed as Uncle Sam
sells flags with his hands on a silver walker
his stump ears like the roots of residual wings
On two stone pillars SHERMAN and FARRAGUT
stand over ANTIETAM and WILDERNESS
and the day's mute ghosts add to the list
My Lai and Hill 192
When someone begins a marching song
three bearded men snap to mock attention
A woman says to a little girl
Come on You know this song Don't you The men
salute and laugh The girl shakes her head no
and ducks and climbs into her father's arms

Migrations

At the foot of the cobbled highway linking
the broad North River to the narrow East
a woman stands on a wooden stool
by the market stalls of beef and wheat
CHOICE NEGROES FROM THE GULF OF GUINEA
naked beside the printed handbill
The citizens squint and negotiate
From where she stands in the swirl of their language
she can see the dock and hear the ships' rigging
and as they peel back her lips from her teeth
she whispers *We whose ancestors traveled*
from desert to the salt water's protection
who fish where the river has many mouths
speak to you Mother of Oceans
This fine cook the merchant is saying
This fine maidservant Her name is Fortune
She closes her eyes *I pour you libations*
goat blood and honey and milk You who make
the fish run thick in the delta channels
the time of the stillness the time of the storms
Where they pinch the skin of her arm she is branded
She shrinks and sways *Here is my calabash*
here the white feathers here the new lamb
Hold my feet while I make my migration
Carry me Here is my song and my dance

Book Four

To The City of Fire

Where are you going Will you leave so quickly
Is the taste of these winter days so bitter
When I whisper to you there is no answer
The night cold has spread all through your sweater
You have snow on your shoulders and no words
    for me
When I listen against your chest I hear
the blurred nightmare sounds of your hindered
    beginnings
drums and the terrible regiments stamping
the silence of waters where nothing lives
What was far has come near The light whittles down
and you are making your hidden decision
What are you looking for Is it here
in the lines at the churches in the hunched crowd's
visible breath in the jabbering mornings
in coins in flats of persimmons in prayer
Will this hearth this soup warm the failing rills
at your throat your temples your lips your wrists
Is it here in my worried footsteps beside you
my starver my staring my less and less
Tell me what song what caress will keep you
I will be apprentice to your dulled tongue
I will kiss your closed eyes I will make shelter
of your tired ribs' smallest movement
sustenance of the warmth of your breathing
continuance of the shreds of your speech

Admirals

The people go naked men and women
of handsome bodies and very good faces
On the first Island I took some by force
that they might give information They remained
so much our friends that it was a marvel
Thus the eternal God our Lord gives
victory to those who follow His way
They swam to the ships and brought us water
They are so free with all they possess
none would believe without having seen it
Of anything they have they give
with as much love as if they gave their hearts
Of keen intelligence they navigate
all these seas but are timid beyond cure
They bear no arms nor know thereof
When I showed them swords they grasped by the
    blade
and cut themselves in ignorance They have
no iron Their spears are made of cane
It seems they belong to no religion
They are of the opinion that I and my ships
come from the source of all power and goodness
the sky In all the world there are no
better people nor better country
With fifty men we could subjugate them
and make them do whatever we want

The Ghost of Santo Domingo

That the earth may shelter and sustain us
that she may wrap herself in mists
and put them off again before us
that she may be everywhere touched by rain
that the planted mounds on the hillside may prosper
that potato and cassava roots
may plunge deep and hold the black earth tightly
that the squash leaves may give moisture and shade
that the island sea may swallow the sun
and with celebration return it to us
that the manatee and its clan may prosper
that the heavy winds may come in their time
that the white sand may warm under the sun's body
and may cool and moisten under the moon
that the moon may navigate its passage safely
that we may gather after the flood tides
that the old rocks may know our newborn children
that the ducklings may know our dying and dead
that in solitude the old ones will protect us
that our songs may travel with the fragrant smoke
that we may smell good to each other
that lovers may laugh and be satisfied
that the village fire burn on unkindled
we face each other and sing without ceasing
We dance We dance We dance We dance

To Peace

Why should you come to meet me your most
awkward lover stumbling over your name
I have nothing to give you I have no way
with gestures or sweetness nothing to say
to those who spit on your likeness before me
nor to those who insist that at last you are dead
nor to you my invisible leaving
your voice in the air when music falls silent
your step on the path when it's too dark to see
your lips on my lips in dreams vanishing
to morning's barren thistles caught in my hair
Here there are many smooth words for you
in all mouths but mine Here you are honored
with banners stained yellow for cowardice
Here boxes of bones are laid at your feet
and rifles thrust into your hands but you
will not hold them I know you by the sound
of the rifles falling and the bones embraced
I am standing between two hills over water
on a narrow log unsure underfoot
You are late and my legs are tired
We share the long night waiting between us
I your devoted impatient stranger
you my skittish near-with-no-sign eyeing
this bridge deciding whether to cross

Our American Way of Life

Chapter Fifteen Our Flag What is this
This is the American Flag
As a new citizen you have a new country
You must pledge allegiance to a new Flag
Every American loves the Flag
There are thirteen stripes in red and white
Next to the staff is a blue field or union
filled with fifty five-pointed white stars
The stars represent a new constellation
Never allow them to touch the ground
Fly the Flag only from sunrise to sunset
Do not use it on handkerchiefs
or paper napkins Pledging Allegiance
Face the Flag Stand at attention
Put your right hand over your heart
A man should hold his hat in his right hand
Answer completely the questions below
Do you know these words Abjure Absolutely
Allegiance Fidelity Potentate Oath
Have you belonged to the Communist Party
Are you a gambler a polygamist
a foreign agent a criminal
Whom do you kiss Have you removed your hat
Fill in the blanks A _____ is a promise
One nation with liberty and _____ for all

At Work

You so sleepy baby Who you been
botherin all night Clarisse laughs She sets
on the green counter eggs triangles of bread
and a gleaming orange glass *She don't say*
nothin she tells her friend I don't answer
She ain't givin nothin away
You better eat up baby She aligns
a knife and fork on the napkin One hand
brushes mine *You hardly holdin up*
that sleepy head She crosses to the window
It's still too early for Saturday's thicket
of orders the row of tickets hung
by the kitchen portal the ache in her feet
She sits at a set table Winter roaring
through the village makes the plate glass tremble
Where your babies at Clarisse her friend calls
and her face changes The smile returns
to the place where she keeps it She rubs her eyes
and doesn't answer *Where your babies today*
her friend calls again They are three
Their photographs grin from the wall by the toasters
I have never met them but I know their names
Girl Clarisse starts She stands and gives me
her square back on the way to the kitchen
to answer *Clarisse Where your babies today*

At School

Merchant and Merchant Junior march
the teeming wharf edge The time has come
to teach the boy the names of the ships
plying the ocean and the salt river
Sloop Schooner Freighter Collier Slaver
Between the palisades Merchant tells him
the Sloop fills his sails On the riverbank
you can stand and halloo and he'll stop for you
to bring flour and lumber and beavers and mail
Sloop Schooner Freighter Collier Slaver
The Schooner's the size of a village he says
the words drawn out by listening *Look there*
That fly by its side is the chandler's tender
He's full of salt fish He's as big as you
Sloop Schooner Freighter Collier Slaver
Down in the Freighter's deep dark holds
his listener shivers *is more molasses*
than you can imagine more cocoa more
biscuits lead soldiers more every good thing
Sloop Schooner Freighter Collier Slaver
The Collier brings coal The Slaver brings slaves
The boy sees a hold full of smiles and eyes
He frowns and skips stones on the water Merchant
has never loved anyone so much
Sloop Schooner Freighter Collier Slaver

Refugees

Until half past eight Pin's daughter belongs
to the pocked concrete walls the puffs of steam
and the piles of pieces she makes into clothing
to the rhythms and roaring of the machines
She walks home more slowly in the summer
to let the warm wind sweep the day from her face
In the tiny apartment the television
mutters advertisements out the window beside
her mother who greets her who cannot see
There was a forest and two great rivers
that Pin's daughter can no longer remember
There was the bombing and there was the lesson
of the stolen rice in the meeting hall
and the beating and then Pin's daughter belonged
to her mother for whom the world disappeared
She cooks fish and rice Her mother nods
and eats and smiles and tells the story
of the leave-taking from Vaisali
At ten o'clock she goes to her room
Pin's daughter's husband who tells riddles
as her father used to but in different words
comes home to share the two night hours
they belong to each other On the couch
he asks the question he has saved for her
She sleeps with the answer waiting on her tongue

Citizens

It is late when she walks from the mica chambers
to meet the others at the café
At the table of coffee and cigarette smoke
they assemble the distant divided city
Each of them carries a piece of it
in the form of a voice The old walled port
of Gaza has its voice the orange trees
the lilies the roses the bougainvillea
the camp sewers and the dysentery
the American tear gas the lemons and grapes
the stones thrown from Jabalia in December
the cemetery cactus and wild cats
the wards of children with broken arms
One brings the voice of demolished houses
one the voice of a map with each village's name
One brings a bruised young woman humming
the forbidden anthem From telephone wires
one brings the tapped voice of the forbidden flag
None of the words of negotiation
none of the strange city's sirens and horns
drowns the voices she guards on each of her shoulders
on one side the stream of words from the young ones
who pass through one Gaza prison room
on the other the breath of an old woman sleeping
who chafes at the rough blanket shaking it off

In That Time

In that time the people gathered at night
to watch the lights in the Palace windows
to ascertain what might become of them
Some stood in all seasons Some called unheard
over tended lawns lacing their fingers
into the grill of the iron gate
Interpreters analyzed the patterns
One light might mean work or hospital beds
Two might mean prisons or houses or war
The King's shadow on a balcony
might mean the fields would again bear fruit
No lights meant the sick kept their corridor vigils
and the young reservists drafted their wills
There was limited participation
in the annual feast called Election Day
In church basements or school gymnasiums
the old and the young with no other employment
guarded booths where citizens stood alone
before machines like those used to gamble
and pulled levers to mark a paper ballot
As the curtain opened the ballot disappeared
The Palace halls were walked only by Princes
The people studied footprints at the gates
The commons were given over to statues
with speechless artillery crouched at their feet

The Shattering

——————————————— *Edward Teller*

We were six We met in the evening
in Wigner's office at Princeton Szilard
recounted the Columbia data
and first spoke about the explosive Bohr
shook his head We tried to convince him
that his openness carried too high a price
He had a green faith in his Physics Republic
But I had seen Horthy when I was a boy
trample the chrysanthemums The day we met
Czechoslovakia lay in pieces
Bohr insisted we would never succeed
in separating the uranium
It can never be done unless you turn
the United States into one huge factory
He said the New Fact might make a New World
if we could keep bootsoles away from its neck
We met past midnight with no conclusions
Years later he came to Los Alamos
with his whispers and his ruined charter
I had no hope of clearing my conscience
I was prepared to tease him *You see*
But before I could open my mouth he said
I told you Now you have your factory
I told him we had that and so much more
He was too wise and would not be comforted

Leviathan

Leviathan scarify and scour
Leviathan leave barren dirt
Leviathan bend you to the diggin
Leviathan stipple lungs with chasms
Leviathan sow fevers and thirst
Leviathan lash-boss the first ones
Leviathan big bellies and flies
Leviathan broadcast sprays of shrapnel
Leviathan spavin all the smallers
Leviathan call it Civilize
Leviathan bill you for the pillage
Leviathan leave you stonybroke
Leviathan counterfeit the bargains
Leviathan oversee the strongbox
Leviathan lock it paper yoke
Leviathan decimate the saplings
Leviathan suck out the pith
Leviathan grind up the seed corn
Leviathan gut the villages
Leviathan say Please Remit
Leviathan wrack the skinny tin-roofs
Leviathan twist the penthouse throat
Leviathan cry like crocodile
Leviathan trick and give mouth honor
Leviathan got the stranglehold

To The Tribunal

———————————— CONGO/ZAIRE

At Léopoldville I stood with the others
to listen He spoke of this struggle of tears
of wounds too fresh to forget His body
had become our body by then That day
the dead by the railroad beds strapped with burdens
by bushes of coffee and copper mines
and the baskets of hands brought for reckoning
were gathered and honored welcome and whole
when he spoke But there was no time for feasting
We were soon carved again into pieces
Three gifts from the Americans came
crates of dollars to buy the garrisons
a rifle in a diplomatic pouch
and a packet of needles and gauze masks
with a vial of poison meant for his tongue
It was his tongue that made them afraid
The world troops sent the gift of protection
We have received many such gifts
The dove hid eagle claws In November
he escaped and tried to reach Stanleyville
On the road we were his pillow his forest
We tore the bridges after he passed
But he was ransomed to the capital
where the new General the Americans' man
with water on only one shoulder by then

folded uniform arms of wood and string
as his men tore the prisoner's declaration
and stuffed the pieces down his throat
Kenyatta had said *I will hold the lion*
so it will not bite Will you bear its claws
but they shackled the thin man's hands behind him
and the lion sent cables across the sea
DEVELOP ANOTHER HORSE TO BACK
HUNTING IS GOOD HERE WHEN SEASON IS RIGHT
This was the blueprint Later the building
covered the land The dead were too many
for us to set them places at the table
In January they took him from his cell
and beat him in the airplane to Katanga
over copper and diamonds gleaming beside
sewer wells and huts of thatch and wood
There was a small house near Elisabethville
Near there a grave had already been dug
Two friends were with him It was days later
before the cry went up in Stanleyville
They have cut out our tongue Lumumba is dead
Hard torches of sun will shine for us
he said Now we are two countries again
Now the trees fall but we have no shelter
Now we harvest but have nothing to eat

Blues

You tell me no trouble's on your trail
You tell me no trouble's on your trail
But you got shakes and blood under your nails

When you keep on lyin like you do
When you keep on lyin like you do
I can't love you the way you want me to

You promised me something you ain't given yet
You promised me Something you ain't given yet
You promised me and I won't forget

Incidents in the Life of a Slave Girl

Dear Amy It has been a long time
since you have seen the scratch of my pen
I was in bed all day yesterday
and could not raise my hands to my head
I am still suffering it in my shoulders
Much sickness in the family this winter
How much I would prize a few hours with you
I have not yet written a single page
by daylight Mornings I am all tablecloths
and sheets and towels and drapery
Mrs Willis is to have Louisa
in exchange for my free winter evenings
but with the care of the little baby
and the big Babies and the multitude
of tiny tasks I have had little time
to think or write In my poor way
I have tried my best and that is not much
and you Friend must not expect much where
there has been so little given I see
at this moment nothing to look forward to
The poor book is in its chrysalis state
I can never make it a butterfly
but would be satisfied to have it creep
meekly among the humbler bugs
I sometimes wish I could fall asleep

Letter March 1854 to Amy Post, abolitionist + ♀'s rights advocate

and wake and believe I was never born
You will say it is too late in the day
that I have outgrown that belief oh yes
and outlived it But I am tired tonight
Sometimes at the head of each city street
I see a black stump In Edenton
in the slave burying ground in the woods
there was a tree my father planted
at the head of my mother's grave before
he lay down beside her When I was last there
it was that black stump I would give anything
to sit this minute on the ground beside it
Have I told you The day my father died
the Mistress was having a spring evening party
I spent the day gathering flowers
and sorting and weaving them into festoons
A mile away he lay dead I long
to see your Rochester trees in bloom
Let no one see this rambling letter
Tonight God's arm is short His ear heavy
I must stop before I weary your patience
Louisa is at my shoulder and sends
her warmest regards to you and your Daisy
Don't expect too much Amy You shall have
no talent but truth Ever your Harriet

Where Blind Sorrow Is Taught To See

Before you I walked with my hands in my pockets
by the dark deserted piers in all weathers
Before you I asked at the oracles
of steel grates and park maples' winter cordage
and tried to decipher the admonitions
of saplings and windows of notebooks and globes
Before you I bluffed and hoarded I ranged
the inconsolable archipelago
bent with useless offerings ungiven
past taverns and perfume and cardboard pallets
longing for the embrace of mannequins
trying to walk captivity's scent
from my clothes Before you I could not hold
oblivion tightly enough against me
The parsed days' murders and educations
settled into the bones of my face
where I could no longer understand them
Before you blank tablets Before you dumb
Before you I looked for you in the rubble
of roadways and broken pediments
in the praying mantis climbing the pilaster
in the bleak hacked view from the promontory
in cuffed new leaves stirring in empty shoes
Before you I walked and whistled invitations
and heard no answering voice before you

Democracy

You bought new clothes You thought it was finished
Your tongue had learned some of the strange new
    words
But the newspapers cry On the stock exchange
the hoarse barkers pace and tear up their tickets
Wake up Wake up We are going to war
Soon all the words will be lost in roaring
and gestures flung into rains of steel
Already the meals are brittled with warnings
the cups set stiffly at the silent places
Push back your chairs We are going to war
It is time to give up the avenues
and pastures you dreamed It is time to take
the strangers whose languages had begun
to touch you and show them who is terrible
and who is afraid We are going to war
We will cast nets over their mouths and bar
all nourishment We will teach the price
of defiance and empty pockets' depth
Your round tables are cinders Put on your boots
and disguises We are going to war
Though they shrink back to their shelters' corners
though they burn their own land under our feet
though generations fall and the birds
drop from the trees we will make dominion
of sand Stand up We are going to war

Soldiers

————————————— *1991*

Come my shirtless my hardly with us
my barefoot my thin my mute torn soldier
Bridegroom Let me caress you Fly over
the land between two rivers the oceans
between us to this warm lit room tonight
Tell my mother you are here She will give you
sweets My father will give you gifts
I know where to cheer your spirit I know
how to gladden your heart Lion Sleep
in our house until dawn Here is salted
flatbread and water Now laugh again Now
show me your teeth and your best jokes Here
are lemon pancakes wrapped in newsprint
rags and a basin a fire in the hearth
for the shreds of your uniform Show me
your dances my alabaster bull
What do we care for stone upon stone
Here are pears and the roots of manna pounded
together Open your lips and drink
Here is the lagoon We the blackheaded
people are the tar-hulled canoe Here are
the reed columns reed rafters the cities of reed
Listen to the ducks' wings in the canebrake
Bridegroom Stretch your silence beside me
Lion Sleep in our house until dawn

Memorials

The cathedral floors and ceiling vaults
join to make one murmur of separate speech
From one central arch hang three faces
in whose names we pour in from the pavements
Michael Schwerner Andrew Goodman James Chaney
The people at the altar have come
from Mississippi to this divided hill
to tell what happened twenty-five years ago
tonight The crowd hides the speakers I hear them
from the walls and see only three faces
James Chaney's in the center To begin
a tenor historian says that the Movement
for which people worked and risked and died
was not of saints or soldiers or kings
but of gardeners kneeling in the mud
to bring forth leaders standing as stakes
for the new life to grow leaning on
pulling the tares bending over the gleanings
faithful through the daily blossoms
and burials in obscurity in danger
In 1961 police killed Herbert Lee
in Liberty Mississippi Lewis Allen
witnessed and told and in '64
was bullet-silenced In June of that year
these three gardeners rode together

CORE
Congress Of Racial Equality: Chaney only black member
Schwerner + Goodman from NYC; S. the leader

on a Sunday night Chaney's grown brother
was a boy then *Mama started a quilt*
the day before the two boys and JE
come up missing She trim old clothes
into patches for the top and leave scraps
for the back stretch the bottom on the floor
then a blanket of cotton then the top
She roll it on a long wood pole On the frame
she stitch and stitch and unroll Most times
it take four days But we kept waiting
and it took a long time The cathedral doors
stand open June sighs in over the stones
part river part caged ailanthus part
work song of a man begging on the steps
part work song of a man inside
Niggers work while the white folks play
What does he care if the land ain't free
and James Chaney's eyes find and rest on mine
and keep them no matter where I look
A memorial a woman says *is*
a covenant I remember singing
this next song three times before
once in the mud in Montgomery holding
my mother's hand once over new graves
in northern Nicaragua and once

at Andrew Goodman's funeral here
Yes I was hoping of course I was
hoping James Chaney's mother says
and he himself says with his eyes I am
from Meridian Neshoba is
Choctaw for wolf On Sunday Mickey
turned right instead of left on 19
Deputy Price took us to jail
in Philadelphia then let us go
On 492 the red light again
and another behind Price at the window
Get out and into his car I saw them
Billy Wayne Posey Jimmy Arledge
Wayne Roberts Doyle Barnette Jordan
On Rock Cut Road Roberts hauled Mickey out
Are you that Jew nigger lover Sir
Mickey said I know just how you feel
and the gun popped blue in his chest and whooping
and Goodman pissing and falling and gone
I was last They lay in a ditch I knew
every face I remember I asked them please
I know what comes now I was born here
Listen The car has no one inside it
Before they drive it into the swamp
before it's burned take it Here are the keys

Migrations

I am wholly ruined Your Highnesses
Within me are only two voyages more
one back to Castile and Your Royal Dominion
one ascending to the right side of Our Lord
We have cheated the jaws of the hurricanes
Late last night as we lay marooned
a messenger came to me in my fever
and spoke to me in the voice of God
Miraculously did He cause thy name
the angel said recounting my blessings
to resound mightily throughout the land
The Indies he gave thee for thine own
and thou hast divided them as it pleased thee
Of the barriers of the Ocean Sea
closed fast with chains He gave you the keys
These keys to gray waters are heavy now
hemmed in by pestilence and corruption
I longed to leave principalities
to my sons There is more I would tell here
but my affliction will not permit it
I am Your vessel Here are Spanish ships
chocked with aloes and cotton and gold
at Your order my Sovereigns We go on
in the name of the Trinity We go on
sending all the slaves that can be sold

Book Five

To The City of Fire

All along there have been places where I
have stopped my sentences to hear you
For every word of this blathering figure
four words' worth of attentive silence This
poem is no more mine than the whorls
of my fingerprints the graves of my ancestors
this Usahn in my mouth and no less Here
is the place for you to speak alive
or dead midwifing this city's birth
or leaving the neckwound cord to its purpose
or sitting by or walking the hallway
outside the red room Here is one place
for you to say your piece although since
we began this journey you have started and stopped
as you pleased put your two cents in
or offered your silence I offer this now
Tell me your part Tell me what I have not
been able to imagine Tell me
the universes parallel to the ones
I know Tell me your ecstatic breakfasts
what food pleases you what gods if any
Tell me your mother and father your sidewalks
and leaves your exiles Tell me what
you have told no one hardly told yourself
Tell me I'm leaning forward to listen

Admirals

Your High Mightinesses I trust you received
word of our autumn calamity
As ice appeared on the river the Tiger
took fire and burned to the waterline
At the end of the Island we built four huts
and passed the winter bickering trade
This post is the proper point whence the furs
could most readily be shipped to Holland
The savages come to the riverbanks
to give fox and otter and beaver pelts
for trinkets and guns I am afraid
I can tell you very little of them
as I have been completely occupied
with the reaping our winter seeds will bring
Today slid down the ways the oak Restless
a staunch yacht of about eight lasts burthen
I expect to explore the Hellgate and the Necks
the savages know on the Island of Shells
Handsome profits could be expected
had we a new Charter from the Cartel
by which we who find new Lands might claim
for four years exclusive trade thereto
I shall bring you back two more sons of chiefs
In the time intervening we remain
Your humble servants of the Company

The Ghost of Santo Domingo

They gave us broken crockery broken
glass the ends of broken straps broken
fragments of hoops that bound the wine casks
red woolen caps hawk's bells glass beads
When he would not set his foot on the land
we swam the cove out to his ship
Some of us he kept and would not let go
We offered pineapples and sweet potatoes
and tried to tell him where the wind was light
and the water fresh and the reefs deeply buried
and where trees spoke storm warnings most clearly
He asked for the ornaments at our necks
We gave bits of gold and rainbow parrots
We embraced him our lost one our brother returned
Before his fort and ruler and compass
before those who touched him fell sick and died
before we stopped lying together to make
no more children before the women set free
from their cabins came back and could not eat or
      sleep
before the withering of the blossomed tree
before we knew them before the unmasking
when their flesh fell away and left fever and swords
we welcomed them We danced and feasted
We ran among the villages calling
Come Come See the people from the sky

To Peace

I have called you names I cannot repeat here
When you have spoken I have turned away
I have kept your every settling place
barren The solace of your absence
has sustained me It is useless now
In the morning you rest on my closed eyelids
and race through neon alphabets at night
Every brick every bus every curb's steel protection
every jackhammer every newspaper hat
every pigeon every furtive night insect
every blighted tree every stranger's breath
brings your hands on my shoulders nearer
my patient tenacious my wide and deep
Your name simmers in the greetings and curses
of the scattered commonwealths of one
We are piecing together your clothes in secret
Those who hide you in rooms underground
who come to the door in their weariness
for your blessing know you by the cooksmoke
over the banked fire by the shards of slate
and chalk by the fretted braids of bread
by the signature of the sentry lichen
over the rocks at the entryway
your sign the slow the ancient the adherent
your emblem the disparate two made one

Our American Way of Life

Chapter Nineteen The People The People
have come to this country for many years
They come from many different places
They come to find freedom They are immigrants
Immigrants have many rights and freedoms
the right to worship and speak and write freely
the right to become citizens who may work
at any job they choose who may own
as much property as they can afford
Every person in the United States is important
Read the stories Answer the questions below
How did Kwok feel when he bought his car
What did Sang think of the food at the diner
Why couldn't Ki buy everything he wanted
When Mai left her country was it raining
Did Mother vote by the secret ballot
Was Sister discussing Current Events
Was there heat in Hortensia's apartment
Could Muhammad live on ten dollars a month
Did Ho understand government by the people
How long did Buchi wait in the line
Does the fog make Mitra sad when she sees it
How many people slept in Jomo's bed
Did Carmen feel good about being trusted
Did Che see the Statue of Liberty's feet

At Work

For where there are no hiding places rows
of women are making hiding clothes
They shift and position the mottled cloth
sealing the seams of the pants and chest pockets
Here is the place his shoulder will rest
here his cock lie along his leg
This will cover his heart and hold what he cannot
carry The blinds tremble with the noise
It is ten at night The trucks are waiting
to carry the order to the depot
The women's fingers fly close to the beating
of each needle's foot Near one locked door
they stack and heft a heavier fabric
The long olive zippers lie in a tray
The finished garments have no arms or legs
but six handles fastened with pounded rivets
Here is where her head will rest and her feet
Here is where her comrades will carry her
When the women stand at the end of the shift
they rub their eyes and stretch and drink
coffee from paper cups so their bodies
will forget it is time to rest They hear
the simmering trucks They calculate
the extra work in diapers and dinners
and resume their places beside the machines

At School

In bright frayed coats and leaping the children
are shepherded to the edge of the cliff
where the powerhouse and the waterfall
lie beside each other and speak
They gather at the feet of a statue
A man with a coat over his arm
stares past the muddy bank grass scattered
with petals to where other people saw
white water spilling down the black rock face
and he saw something else The children watch him
and read together from the pedestal
TO ALEXANDER HAMILTON
WHOSE VISION MADE THIS VERY GROUND
THE CRADLE OF INDUSTRY They follow
his gaze The powerhouse is surrounded
by barbed wire the windows meshed with chain
the water's voice barely audible
under the turbines' churning The robins
light on branches stammering into green
beside the bridge The steadfast traffic
crosses to and from the haggard town
Two voices ripple and whirr The children
standing on blossoms listen to them
one metronomic one everchanging
one consuming one almost consumed

Refugees

At midnight the old year blows its cold breath
for the last time at the windows that shelter
the exiled dancers They lift their glasses
and kiss each other With the new year has come
word from the city of the end of the war
The dancers far from the battlegrounds
search each other for signs of the new world
the new year has made One man with tears
on his cheeks calls a toast *To the paper peace*
May we learn to eat it and make it flesh
A woman with scars between her fingers
toasts *The peace of the fluttering wings*
May we see the bird fly To the magic dogs
who protect us we of the black volcanoes
To the signatures and the courtesy
To the peace of this small flame May we learn
to tend and feed it To the peace of this stone
on this steep mountainside May we brace it
and build our country on its foundation
To the soldiers who sit and lay down their weapons
To the dead who dance with us tonight
There is no sleep for them but there is rest
The dawn is cold and brings no safety
but no end to the dancing and the embraces
that hold the green hope and the nearness to home

Citizens

In the bars and private rooms of the city
the exiles and citizens sit together
and spread across the table before them
the new maps of the lands where their ancestors lie
In Budapest the man who was hanged
and buried facedown in an unmarked grave
is turned and given his ceremony
In Warsaw the tin speech is quieted
and the delicate code of fables broken
The city echoes with the shipyards' speech
In Sofia and Vilnius the banners gape
the emblems cut out leaving only the colors
In Bucharest amid lamentation
troops are sent to cut down a poplar tree
hung with pears The Tin King has said change
    will come
when the weeds blossom and the poplars bear fruit
The springtime of nations has come in winter
The cold squares are empty of helplessness
The scientists and the pipefitters
the playwright and the electrician
stand on land the Armies trampled between them
littered with secrets and threats and reprisals
with the bodies of poisoned rivers and trees
and of citizens who are lifted now
and given roses and their rightful names

In Berlin in the ecstasy of the Reunion
those arrested and kicked in the mud courtyard
forced to stand facing the stones all night
scale the Wall before the bulldozers breach it
to kiss strangers' cheeks on the other side
There is dancing where each rough new gate appears
Where there were guards there are cutters of wire
hammers and chisels a cello a chair
The Empire opens its tin fingers
and gives back the conquered privacies
In Moscow the monoliths are pulled down
and replaced with the old quarrels' babble
taken up again after the time of gagging
of blindfolds and bound wrists and broken teeth
In Prague the people make the stones tremble
They call to the soldiers *We have bare hands*
They gather The president of forgetting
is stripped of forum and obedience
A man with a different voice takes his place
Across the ocean in bars and kitchens
the people lift their glasses to him
After the joy of unmaking he tells them
comes the difficult work to provide to build
For better or worse rich or poor my people
your government is returned to you

In That Time

In that time the people presided over
what came to be known as The Great Dying
Osprey and herons and hawks were exchanged
for speedboats and paved wooden neighborhoods
Bear and beaver and moose disappeared
for top hats and gas pumps to take their places
The gifts to the seventh generation
included dead fish piled in simmering creeks
tides that bore surgical sutures and needles
horizons heavy with smokestacks and tailpipes
falling on trees as searing rain
The earth was opened for interment of poisons
The sky was divided by lots and sold
The sounds that the wind and rain made together
became audible only in fenced preserves
Unprecedented prosperity
sustained the industries of destruction
the makers of stacks of prison cages
of chairs designed for electrocution
of weapons to suppurate the deserts
and erase waterlines and warehouses of seeds
A banner of that time depicts many children
standing on top of a map of the world
Some smile Some stare without expression
at the thicket of swords hanging over their heads

The Shattering

The President and the Prime Minister
confer by the river in the autumn
In two empty chairs sit two other guests
a prophet and a conflagration
On Sunday the President drives so close
to the edge of the wooded palisade cliffs
that the Prime Minister loses all his color
Only wholeness leads to clarity Let
*the informed enemies stand facing each othe*r
On Monday the servants clear the dishes
and the women and children disappear
The President and the Prime Minister
We are in a completely new situation
that cannot be resolved by war
sequester themselves in one small stuffy room
They peruse the partitioned continent
spread flat on the round table before them
before turning to the delicate subject
of prophecy *This is not a weapon*
This is a deeper interference
than anything ever before attempted
The Prime Minister's flush has returned to him
Who is this Mr Unarmed Republic
this great advocate of publicity
this allergic to secrets this saboteur

this treason with his hair all over his head
In one empty chair the prophet pales
We did not even speak the same language
and the conflagration hisses and flickers
as the President's silence pleads its suit
He gazes out over his property
and wishes for something cool to drink
In a blaze of friendship the two compose
a memorandum at the end of the day
The suggestion that the world be informed
with a view to international agreement
is not accepted Utmost secrecy
will continue Every sentence I utter
is to be understood as a question
When available the bomb might be used
against the Japanese who should be warned
that this will continue until they surrender
As for Professor Bohr enquiries
should be made Privately they agree
perhaps August if the weather is fine
From one of the empty chairs there is silence
They draw the other into their circle
and mark the bridges and delta islands
and shallow canals of the wooden city
with a handshake and a cross of fire

Leviathan

Leviathan the bullet bulwark
Leviathan squat on death silos
Leviathan unstint the onslaught
Leviathan give no benison
Leviathan wear the Führer clothes
Leviathan deal poppies and coca
Leviathan buy guns for sale
Leviathan blur the money faces
Leviathan the laundry expert
Leviathan strafe it flimflam trail
Leviathan Dean of Wooden Legs
Leviathan the Orphan King
Leviathan engineer of craters
Leviathan the soldier vendor
Leviathan lie you what it bring
Leviathan ventriloquist
Leviathan prestidigitate
Leviathan make assemblies rackets
Leviathan slit question committees
Leviathan interrogate
Leviathan the Ribcage Regent
Leviathan the Ashes Lord
Leviathan Chancellor of the Boneyard
Leviathan make the folk spit bitter
Leviathan Conquistador

To The Tribunal

———————————————— *INDONESIA*

To protect ourselves we had knives and bamboo
spears We felled trees But we were not
an army When the soldiers came in trucks
In Java there is no place out of sight
or hearing When the soldiers came in trucks
I hid The people were made to dig
and fell forward and their names were checked off
Suharto the Americans' man
had lists of names they made for him
They called this Civic Action Piked heads
lined the streets without flowers or feasting
The most common grave was the river Before
this time in the villages the people made
the irrigation with bamboo and stones
make music with the water's passage
By December barriers had to be built
to bar the bodies as they drifted to sea
each bound to bamboo to float to send
a message The small rivers choked this way
In the shadow play Arjuna who lives
without sleep who trembles at the killing
of kinsmen sees the heroes' heads crushed
between the god's jaws In the villages
the people sit on both sides of the screen
They see the shadows and the masters behind

Blues

By this fire I still can feel the wind
By this fire I still can feel the wind
Stays by my shoulders like it's listenin

All night I hear somebody callin me
All night I hear somebody callin me
But I can't think what could the answer be

When I get home I'll lock the peaceful in
When I get home I'll lock the peaceful in
When I get home I'll tell you where I been

Incidents in the Life of a Slave Girl

June 1867 Dear Amy
I am two days returned from Edenton
I cannot tell you how I felt there
The change is too great to take it all in
My grandmother's house still stands on King Street
For me there was solace in every timber
I loved to sit there and think of her
to think of them all It was a hard winter
The freedmen were cheated out of their cotton
I spent many hours on the plantations
distributing seed hunting up the old people
and doing what I could for them
Now it is back to carpets and mantels
Louisa has been living on Long Island
as a governess to a twelve-year-old girl
She seems to like her situation
but I miss her very much indeed
I must stop It is very late
and I am in the only spot
where I can have a light The mosquitoes
have gathered and taken possession of me
My love to Miss Daisy Did she receive
the jasmine blossoms I sent her from there
Tell her they bear the fragrance of freedom
Believe me the same always Harriet

Where Blind Sorrow Is Taught To See

Near where I lived there was a fenced schoolyard
where at night the bloody ghost children played
calling in all the languages
I never saw them there again after
that night on the small curved street when you
    kissed me
Past the screen door where the late dishwashers
stood to smoke past the young woman sitting
on two overturned milk crates sorting roses
with bats of her fingers coaxing the curled buds
open you stood me against the dark bricks
and kissed me insisting your tongue quick and sweet
Why were you not afraid as I was
Why was there no forbidden place
You held me and opened my shirt and touched me
in the building's shadow where no one could see
All evening I had watched you lifting
wooden sticks over the plate of pods
and blossoms your eager reaching to open
oranges and folded futures What were
the words I whispered Your legs held
mine apart Did I tell you everything
You pushed your fingers inside me Sorrow
hovered and found no lighting place
its bruised cheeks healed with your lips' attention
its restless thirst watered and soothed to rest

Democracy

This is the sowing time The harvest
will come when the last of the kings is dead
Now we will sing We will splint the body
of broken bones and light candles together
The stitchers and fasteners of buttons
leave work today to walk in the rain
with the servers of soup and pressers of sheets
down the blighted city's gray avenues
behind caskets filled with incense and fruit
The shopkeepers empty rain from the awnings
and furl them and fasten the shutters and grates
for the time it takes the mourners to pass
the boys' heads wrapped in white handkerchiefs
the hairdressers' black ribbons pinned to their coats
The lost builders of the ragged city
of hope in the distant square now empty
travel with the marchers in the rain Here
the bloody stretchers are no longer hidden
The people link mourning arms and remember
the bicycles the torn jackets the names
of those who kept the hard vigil who turned
frightened private silences into speech
Here their words are spoken again *You are*
ours You are our brothers and sisters
The people's army must not crush the people

Soldiers

In the mica chambers the princes sit
before their blotters and glasses of water
The doors are closed In the corridors
lie burned rice bowls and school uniforms
The silent bell waits in the winter garden
Men in overcoats walk by the river
gesturing toward the island of ruins
the rubbled meadows the distant smokestacks
the derricked barges kicking up yellow spray
In the courtyard among the stripped fruit trees
stands a green man his chest and face streaming
naked one hand raising a blunt mallet
one bracing what once was the blade of a sword
His face is not humble or knowing or joyful
It is a soldier's face the lips closed
only the steeply arched eyebrows betraying
the weight of what he has been made to do
WE SHALL BEAT OUR SWORDS INTO
    PLOWSHARES it says
on the pedestal But what he has made
so far is only a useless weapon
a broken thing he does not recognize
The princes in the hierarchies
of the bullied councils bicker and contend
He faces the chambers but does not see them
He bows his head He bends to his work

Memorials

This afternoon cut bound shocks of cane
lean against open-backed vans on upper
Broadway In back are coconuts hacked
to the sweet white meat with machetes Sweat
darkens the sides of the shirts of the men
who hand out cups of iced juice from plantains
and pike oranges beside mounted blades
their peels spun away in one continuous
curving Up the street past red white and blue
ice rockets papayas and soaps called Dove
and Shield on the hill is the stone museum
MAYA CARIB ARAWAK in the sky
ALGONQUIN SHOSHONE IROQUOIS SIOUX
and over Quixote's starving horse
and broken spear PIZARRO CORTES
DE LEON PINZON COLUMBUS Inside
past the cashier silenced sealed in glass
is a beaded condolence string with the deaths
of twenty chiefs nicked in the pendant
Belts of quahog wampum tell histories
in a language of raised arms and evergreens
A Cherokee sculptor from North Carolina
in loafers and patience a bear claw hung
from his neck carves faces from rock *Pleased*
to meet you two women say to a third

gesturing toward the sculptor *We have*
a boy on his reservation We wanted
an American What were we gonna get
a ghetto kid No sir We decided
on a Native American and no sir
we've never regretted it One opens
a wallet and takes out a photograph
He's fourteen now taller than me He's planning
a military career From a wall
Buffalo Bill smiles his hired smile
The chisel rings The Annual Report
of the Minnesota State Treasurer
July 4 1863 records
that from the Military Expense Fund
J C Davis paid for Postage Stamps
Canisters Transportation of Arms
Labor in Arsenal Powder and Lead
and Sioux Scalps as per the order that offered
twenty-five dollars *to anybody*
for each scalp of a male Sioux delivered
to this office There is a case of hair
Two tourists speaking German look
and nod and murmur the tribal names
The cards beside the cases speak
but do not say *On the day when the people*

understand who you were they will bite the earth
*and raise to you temple*s They name a dusty
race of strangers with no connection
to we who step onto Broadway and walk
over the ravaged land At the hatches
of the vans bearing fruits of the island
the Admiral gulled and gutted and changed
forever the children of former slaves
and the children of former slaveowners
and the children of their commingling greet
each other in the tongue of the conquerors
and in its rebellious variations
Babies sleep in strollers their large lolled heads
at right angles to their narrow shoulders
Their bodies and later the crescent moon's
blurred cusps testify beside the forges
and furnace smokestacks and sirens and trains
that this island is not a machine Inside
the locked museum the corner is dark
that describes the Taino those who taught Columbus
how to feed himself and his men how to sleep
in net beds hung between trees or hold hooks
Taino was their word for themselves It was
a word they spoke to strangers It was
a greeting meaning people of peace

Migrations

It was the moon of big winds In the night
I dreamed the dance at the death of a chief
We have put his things in their places we sang
in the Circle *We have wiped the blood*
from the earth where he stood his abiding place
We have smoothed over the earth where he lay
Then the new chief stepped forward but his face
was hidden *Now the council fire*
is rekindled we sang to him dancing *The sorrow*
we have borne it elsewhere From your throat
we have taken the grief You have lost
that upon which your eyes rested trustfully
Nevertheless there are many matters
Now the commonwealth rests in your hands
The morning was clear But all day the dream
walked beside me The leaves of the tallest trees
spoke its words and held its hidden face
By the stream rocks we washed in the glinting sprays
Over the water the sun swept to warm us
Over the water the birds swept to eat
Over the water the wind swept to hurry
the end of the day's harvest Before dark
I slept again between two trees I saw
over the water the sweep of gulls' wings
over the water a signal a sail

MAY 1988–JANUARY 1992

Notes

The New World is centered in the circle fifty miles in all directions from Columbus Circle in Manhattan. The messages from other parts of the world are transmitted through this geographical area; the only exceptions are the voice of Columbus and that of the Ghost of Santo Domingo, speaking from where they first encountered each other, five hundred years ago.

In the poem, many voices speak; my name on it should not be understood as any claim to originality or ownership. I am less the poem's author than its gatherer; to make it, I "thought" much less than I listened. In the words of a Chilean song, "Yo no soy quien canto, solo soy la voz." The list of sources below is far from complete.

Book One

"The Ghost of Santo Domingo," page 5 and thereafter. See Kirkpatrick Sale, *The Conquest of Paradise* (New York: Knopf, 1990) and Howard Zinn, *A People's History of the United States* (New York: HarperCollins, 1980).

"Our American Way of Life," page 7 and thereafter. These sections are based on U.S. government publications on preparing for citizenship, particularly one called *Our American Way of Life*, now no longer in use.

"Citizens," page 11. *Usahn* is a homemade synonym for *American*.

"The Shattering," page 13. See Laura Fermi, *Atoms in the Family: My Life with Enrico Fermi* (Albuquerque: University of New Mexico Press, 1954). This section takes place in 1939. Throughout, see Richard Rhodes, *The Making of the Atomic Bomb* (New York: Simon & Schuster, 1986).

"To The Tribunal," page 16. See the testimony of Olga Mejía of the Human Rights Commission of Panama, on the news program "Undercurrents," WBAI, New York, during the week of February 22, 1991. These sections are imagined accounts of a tribunal on United States intervention in the histories of other nations.

"Incidents in the Life of a Slave Girl," page 18 and thereafter. See Harriet Jacobs, *Incidents in the Life of a Slave Girl*, ed. Jean Fagan Yellin (Cambridge: Harvard University Press, 1987). In the course of trying to escape a master threatening her with rape, Harriet Jacobs hid in a small garret above a storeroom in her grandmother's house for seven years.

"Soldiers," page 22. "The casualties at Antietam numbered four times the total suffered by American soldiers at the Normandy beaches on June 6, 1944. More than twice as many Americans lost their lives in one day at Sharpsburg as fell in combat in the War of 1812, the Mexican War, and the Spanish-American War combined." (James McPherson, *Battle Cry of Freedom*, Oxford: Oxford University Press, 1988).

"Migrations," page 24. This is an imagined song before history, sung in the wake of the last glacial retreat. See Bruce G. Trigger, ed., *Handbook of North American Indians*, vol. 15, (Washington D.C.: Smithsonian, 1978).

Book Two

"Admirals," page 29. Verrazano's voyage to the mouth of the Hudson took place in April 1524, in the service of France. This section is based on his account. On a later voyage, Verrazano was seized by the people of a Caribbean island in the Lesser Antilles and killed.

"Citizens," page 37. Malcolm X was shot and killed in the Audobon Ballroom in 1965. That night a Brooklyn civic group held a dance there. The lines quoted at the end of this section are based on a speech called "Some Reflections on 'Negro History Week' and the Role of Black People in History." The part that follows refers to the building of the pyramids: "Before you and I came over here, we were so well balanced we could toss something on our head and run with it. You can't even run with your hat now—you can't keep it on. Because you lost your balance. You've gotten away from yourself. But when you are in tune with yourself, your very nature has harmony, has rhythm, has mathematics. You can build. You don't even need anybody to teach you how to build. You play music by ear. You dance by how you're feeling. And you used to build the same way. You have it in you to do it." (John Henrik Clarke, ed., *Malcolm X: The Man and His Times* [New York: Macmillan, 1969].)

"The Shattering," page 39 Stanislaw Ulam was a Polish mathematician who made central contributions to the creation of both the atomic and the hydrogen bomb. The Sieve of Eratosthenes is a systematic arrangement of prime numbers. This section takes place in 1939.

"To The Tribunal," page 42. See Douglas Valentine, *The Phoenix Program* (New York: Morrow, 1990).

"Soldiers," page 48. This section is an imagined aftermath to the massacres at Pavonia in 1643, where New Amsterdam governor Willem Kieft and his troops killed and mutilated 1,500 Wappinger Indians who had fled there for protection from Mohawk raids. The reference at the end is to a custom of burial: sitting up, facing east.

"Migrations," page 52. The people who lived on Long Island and Manhattan when the first Europeans arrived made frequent migrations westward, to flee persecution.

Book Three

"Admirals," page 56. Hudson's voyage took place in October 1609, under the auspices of the Amsterdam Charter of the Dutch East India Company. On his last voyage, he was stranded for a difficult winter in the course of exploring what is now Hudson's Bay; in June 1611, crew members seized him, his son and several others and set them adrift in a small boat without provisions.

"The Shattering," page 65. Herbert Anderson was the first person in the United States to create and observe nuclear fission, at Columbia University in January, 1939.

"To The Tribunal," page 69. Between 1979 and 1990, in violation of U.S. and international law, the United States government secretly created an army and supplied it with weapons in order to overthrow the government of Nicaragua. See Leslie Cockburn, *Out of Control: The Story of the Reagan Administration's Secret War in Nicaragua, the Illegal Arms Pipeline, and the Contra Drug Connection* (New York: Atlantic Monthly Press, 1987).

"Soldiers," page 74. During five days and nights of open battle between Newark police and black citizens in Newark in July 1967, police killed William Furr, twenty-four years old, and with the same shotgun blast wounded Joe Bass, Jr., twelve years old, at the corner of Avon and Livingston. See Dale Wittner, "Newark: The Predictable Insurrection," *Life*, vol. 63, no. 4, July 28, 1967.

"Memorials," page 75. Hill 192 was the site of the abduction, rape, and murder of a Vietnamese woman by United States soldiers. See Daniel Lang, *Casualties of War* (New York: McGraw-Hill, 1969).

"Migrations," page 77. In 1734 a slave market stood at the foot of Wall Street, on the East River. See Frederick Trevor Hill, *The Story of a Street* (Burlington: Fraser Publishing Company, 1969).

Book Four

"Admirals," page 82. See Cecil Jane, trans., *The Journal of Christopher Columbus* (New York: Clarkson Potter, 1960).

"Refugees," page 88. The land of the forest and two great rivers is Cambodia. The story of the leave-taking from Vaisali comes from the *Buddhacarita* or "The Acts of the Buddha," by the first century Indian poet Ashvaghosha. In the story, Buddha looks on the town of Vaisali and says, "O Vaisali, this is the last time that I see you. For I am now departing for Nirvana!" See Edward Conze, trans., *Buddhist Scriptures* (New York: Penguin, 1959).

In 1969 the U.S. began secret bombing raids into neutral Cambodia. In 1970, U.S. ground troops invaded from Vietnam. By 1972, two million Cambodians had been made homeless by the war. The bombing of Cambodia continued until 1973. In those four years, 539,129 tons of U.S. bombs were dropped there. Under Pol Pot, in the war's aftermath, an estimated two million Cambodians died. See William Shawcross, *Sideshow: Kissinger, Nixon and the Destruction of Cambodia* (New York: Simon & Schuster, 1979).

"Citizens," page 89. The intifada began in Jabalia in December, 1987. The word's literal translation from Arabic is "the shaking off." See Gloria Emerson, *Gaza/A Year in the Intifada: A Personal Account* (New York: Atlantic Monthly Press, 1991).

"The Shattering," page 91. In 1919 Admiral Nicholas Horthy rode into Budapest and installed a violent fascist regime, the first in Europe. Edward Teller was eleven years old. Chrysanthemums were the symbol of the short-lived 1918 Hungarian revolution.

The last line here was spoken not by Teller but by Robert Oppenheimer. The section is set in 1939.

"To The Tribunal," page 93. See Madeleine G. Kalb, *The Congo Cables: The Cold War in Africa from Eisenhower to Kennedy* (New York: Macmillan, 1982) and *Patrice Lumumba* (London: Panaf Books, 1978). Lines five through seven refer to the killings and mutilations carried out during the eighty-year colonial regime under Belgium. "The Americans' man" is Joseph Mobutu, later Mobutu Sese Seko. Lumumba was the only leader of Congo/Zaire ever elected by its people.

"Soldiers," page 100. This section is based on translations of documents and poetry from ancient Mesopotamia. See Samuel Noah Kramer, *Cradle of Civilization* (Alexandria: Time-Life Books, 1978). In 1991 an estimated 100,000 Iraqi soldiers were killed by U.S. military forces in the course of the largest bombing mission in history.

"Migrations," page 104. The voice here is Columbus's, based on his Journal.

Book Five

"To The City of Fire," page 107. *Usahn* refers here to the Englishes spoken in the United States.

"Admirals," page 108. Adriaen Block's exploration of Long Island Sound and southern New England took place in 1613. Block Island is named for him. In 1614 the Dutch merchants who financed his explorations organized the New Netherland Company, and obtained from the States General a monopoly on the fur trade in the region between the 40th and 45th parallels. See B. Fernow, *Documents Relating to the Colonial History of the State of New York* (Albany: The Argus Company, 1877).

"At School," page 113. The waterfall is where the Passaic River flows through Paterson, New Jersey.

"Refugees," page 114. An important part of the final peace agreements between the U.S.-backed government of El Salvador and the FMLN guerilla resistance was signed at about midnight on the last day of 1991. Between 1979 and 1991, more than 70,000 Salvadoran civilians were killed by U.S.-backed military and paramilitary death squads. The magic dogs are *cadejos*, who protect the people of the volcanoes from danger. See *El Salvador's Decade of Terror*, Americas Watch (New Haven: Yale University Press, 1991), and Manlio Argueta, *Magic Dogs of the Volcanoes* (San Francisco: Children's Book Press, 1990).

"Citizens," page 115. The man in Budapest is Imre Nagy. The shipyards' speech is that of the Solidarity workers of Gdansk. The phrase "the president of forgetting" comes from Milan Kundera. The final quotes are based on the inauguration speech of Vaclav Havel on January 1, 1990. He said, "My most important predecessor started his first speech by quoting from Comenius. Permit me to end my own first speech by my own paraphrase. Your Government, my people, has returned to you."

"The Shattering," page 118. In September 1944 Roosevelt and Churchill met at Hyde Park. Among other things, they discussed Neils Bohr's plea that the U.S. reveal the details of its atomic bomb construction to the Soviet Union, to prevent a disastrous postwar arms race. Churchill's deep suspicion of Bohr won out, and the two drafted the quoted memorandum together. See Ruth E. Moore, *Neils Bohr: The Man, His Science, and the World They Changed* (New York: Knopf, 1966).

"To The Tribunal," page 121. See Peter Dale Scott, *Coming to Jakarta* (New York: New Directions, 1988), and Brian May, *The Indonesian Tragedy* (New York: Routledge Kegan Paul, 1978).

"Democracy," page 125. The scene is a march in Manhattan; the "distant square now empty" is Tiananmen, where in the spring of 1989 Chinese students and other citizens gathered to demonstrate for democracy. The square was violently cleared by the army on June 4, with many killed. The quoted words at the end are the demonstrators', spoken to the soldiers.

"Soldiers," page 126. The burned bowls and uniforms are on display at the United Nations in memory of the victims of the atomic bombs dropped on Hiroshima and Nagasaki. The bell is a peace bell donated by Japan, which is rung only on the opening day of the General Assembly and on the first day of spring.

"Memorials," page 127. The quotation beginning with "On the day when the people" is based on an inscription by Vercors at the Memorial to the Unknown Deported in Paris: *"Mais le jour où les peuples auront compris qui vous étiez ils mordront la terre de chagrin et de remords ils l'arroseront de leurs larmes et ils vous éleveront des temples."*

"Migrations," page 130. The last voice is that of the Ghost of Santo Domingo. The quoted lines are based on a traditional ceremony of condolence.

Acknowledgments

The author and publisher wish to express their grateful acknowledgment to the following publications in which some sections of this poem first appeared, often in different versions:

The American Voice
"Admirals" (Book One), formerly "The Admiral"
"Where Blind Sorrow Is Taught to See" (Book One)
"Where Blind Sorrow Is Taught to See" (Book Three)

Grand Street
"At School" (Book One), formerly "Two Boys"
"Memorials" (Book Two), formerly "The West"
"Point Museum"
"The Shattering" (Book One)
"The Shattering" (Book Two)
"The Shattering" (Book Three)

The Kenyon Review—New Series, Summer 1991, Vol. XIII, No. 3.
"To The City of Fire" (Book Two), formerly "To the Strangers"
"To Peace" (Book One), formerly "To Justice"
"To Peace" (Book Two)
"To The Tribunal" (Book One)

The Paris Review
"Our American Way of Life" (Book One) and "At Work" (Book Two) were published under the title "Citizens."

Pequod
"To The City of Fire" (Book One), "To The City of Fire" (Book Three), "Memorials" (Book One), and "Citizens" (Book One) were published under the title "From THE NEW WORLD."

Ploughshares
"The Ghost of Santo Domingo" (Book Two), formerly "1494"

"Incidents in the Life of a Slave Girl" (Book One), formerly "1853"

TriQuarterly, a publication of Northwestern University
"Memorials" (Book Five), formerly "Museum of the American Indian"

Several sections of the poem were first published in *Usahn: Ten Poems & A Story* (Grand Street Books, 1990).

About the Author ——————

Suzanne Gardinier was born in 1961 in New Bedford, Massachusetts, and grew up in Scituate, on the coast south of Boston. She attended the University of Massachusetts (B.A., 1981) and Columbia University (M.F.A., 1986), and has taught writing at SUNY Old Westbury, Rutgers/Newark, and several other colleges, as well as in the New York City public schools. Since 1988 she has lived with Georgia Heard in Sag Harbor, New York. She is currently at work on a novel called *The Seventh Generation*.

PITT POETRY SERIES

Ed Ochester, General Editor

Archibald MacLeish, *The Great American Fourth of July Parade*

Peter Meinke, *Liquid Paper: New and Selected Poems*

Peter Meinke, *Night Watch on the Chesapeake*

Carol Muske, *Applause*

Carol Muske, *Wyndmere*

Leonard Nathan, *Carrying On: New & Selected Poems*

Ed Ochester and Peter Oresick, *The Pittsburgh Book of Contemporary American Poetry*

Sharon Olds, *Satan Says*

Alicia Suskin Ostriker, *Green Age*

Alicia Suskin Ostriker, *The Imaginary Lover*

Greg Pape, *Black Branches*

Greg Pape, *Storm Pattern*

Kathleen Peirce, *Mercy*

David Rivard, *Torque*

Liz Rosenberg, *Children of Paradise*

Liz Rosenberg, *The Fire Music*

Maxine Scates, *Toluca Street*

Richard Shelton, *Selected Poems, 1969–1981*

Betsy Sholl, *The Red Line*

Peggy Shumaker, *The Circle of Totems*

Peggy Shumaker, *Wings Moist from the Other World*

Jeffrey Skinner, *The Company of Heaven*

Leslie Ullman, *Dreams by No One's Daughter*

Constance Urdang, *Alternative Lives*

Constance Urdang, *Only the World*

Ronald Wallace, *The Makings of Happiness*

Ronald Wallace, *People and Dog in the Sun*

Belle Waring, *Refuge*

Michael S. Weaver, *My Father's Geography*

Robley Wilson, *Kingdoms of the Ordinary*

Robley Wilson, *A Pleasure Tree*

David Wojahn, *Glassworks*

David Wojahn, *Mystery Train*

Paul Zimmer, *Family Reunion: Selected and New Poems*